Strategic Finance for Strategic Leaders:
The First Five Tools

STRATEGIC
FINANCE
for Strategic Leaders
The First Five Tools

Rick Mann, PhD
David Tarrant, MBA

Strategic Finance for Strategic Leaders: The First Five Tools
By Rick Mann, PhD and David Tarrant, MBA

Published by: ClarionStrategy LLC, Nashville, TN

www.ClarionStrategy.com
www.ClarionToolBox.com

DEDICATION

To all the leaders and managers out there who seek to
create value every day through the skilled use of financial resources.

TABLE OF CONTENTS

ClarionToolBox Series

Strategic Leaders Are Made, Not Born: The First Five Tools for Escaping the Tactical Tsunami by Rick Mann

Building Strategic Organizations: The First Five Tools of Strategy and Strategic Planning by Rick Mann

Coaching: The First Tools For Strategic Leaders (coming 2020) by Rick Mann)

Enterprise Leaders: The First Five FIELD Tools (coming 2021) by Rick Mann and Dean Diehl

ACKNOWLEDGMENTS

Thanks to the many who have spoken into the development of this book.

Thanks to our university leadership teams at Belhaven and Trevecca who have supported our work on this project. Thanks to our series editor, Kara de Carvalho, and series designer, Lieve Maas.

Special thanks to all of the supervisors and co-workers we have had over the years who have pushed us to improve and challenged us to bring our best work every day. As we look back, we are thankful for how they have shaped us to become more strategic, intentional and graceful as we face today's business climate.

PREFACE

I [Rick] am writing this section in March of 2020, as news about the COVID-19 coronavirus is everywhere. Its impact on the US and on the world is pervasive. After discussions around the number of tests, cases, and deaths, the conversation inevitably turns to the economy. Companies and organizations everywhere are concerned about cash. Yes, as you will read later, cash is the lifeblood of every organization. Without cash, you can't keep operating.

When unexpected things hit, a solid understanding of the financial basics is even more important than ever. I had a conversation with my university president last week during which he assured us that we had enough cash to meet our payroll. Cash gets very practical very quick when it comes to determining whether we will get paid or not.

Meet David Tarrant

I remember interviewing David Tarrant as a CFO (Chief Financial Officer) candidate at Crown College like it was yesterday.

"What are you doing now?" I asked him.

"I am a senior finance officer for the Whirlpool brand," he replied.

"What is the size of that budget?" I continued.

"Two billion dollars," he said, without batting an eye.

"That's big enough for us!" I exclaimed as I thought of our budget, which was around $20 million.

After acing his interview, David got the job. Once he started working at Crown College, I found myself constantly telling people, "Even though he makes more than $100K, David would be a great value even if we paid him twice as much. He finds a new way to strategically save us a million dollars each year."

Thus began a personal and professional friendship that has lasted more than a decade. Over the years, I have learned so much from David about the practical and strategic features of accounting and finance. The son of an accounting professor, David has a knack for explaining financial issues to people who are not financial professionals. He helps people make sense of the numbers. This skill, along with his quick smile, have led to his professional success wherever he has worked across his 30+ years as a financial professional and 12+ years as a CFO at a number of organizations.

Some years ago, I saw the need for this book. At the same time, I knew that I could only write it with David's insight. Our goal here is to help you and those on your team to think more strategically about finance.

Suggested Reading

If you have not already done so, I would suggest that you read the first two books in this ClarionToolBox series:

Strategic Leaders Are Made, Not Born: The First Five Tools for Escaping the Tactical Tsunami by Rick Mann (2019, ClarionStrategy).

Building Strategic Organizations: The First Five Tools for Strategy and Strategic Planning by Rick Mann (2019, ClarionStrategy).

These books will give you some insight and a framework that will extend the concepts learned in this book. When you better understand creating value, TEMP resources, and ROI, this book will make more sense.

PPO Approach

Every tool listed in this series is designed to be applied to both life and work. I call this the "PPO approach." I use the PPO approach in each of my books and graduate courses because my goal is for you to apply every tool that you learn in the following areas:

- Personal
- Professional
- Organizational

The late Clay Christensen, a professor at Harvard Business School and the acclaimed author of *The Innovator's Dilemma* (1997), detailed the PPO approach in his book, *How Will You Measure Your Life?* (2012). I have my MBA students read his 6-page *Harvard Business Review* article (2010) by the same title, while my DBA students read the full book.

My hope for you is that you can win at life AND win at work. The result can be a flourishing personal and family life as well as a thriving organization.

GOLDEN CIRCLE

The WHY, HOW, and WHAT Framework

As I mentioned in *Strategic Leaders Are Made, Not Born*, I draw on some of the material from the Golden Circle model popularized by Simon Sinek, author of *Start With Why* (2009). As of 2020, his TED talk on this subject was the 4th most-watched TED talk, with about 50 million views. In his work, Sinek talks about three circles: Why, How, and What. He expounds on why companies do what they do. He then discusses how companies do what they do. Lastly, he talks about what companies do. I have adapted this framework to my work here, following the same outline for each of the five tools listed in this book.

WHY It Matters – First, we look at why the tool matters. This includes the importance of understanding the concepts and putting them into practice. I also explain why things go poorly when the tool is neglected.

HOW It Works – Next, we unpack the main concepts that are central to the particular tool.

WHAT to Do Next? – Lastly, I suggest how you can put the tool to use in your personal life, your professional life, and your organizational life (PPO).

This simple "why, how, and what" framework can help you learn and apply each tool more quickly.

INTRODUCTION

"Rick, why would you want to get an MBA?" a friend of mine asked me in 2005.

"Because I can't even spell P&L [Profit and Loss Statement]," I replied. "As a CEO, I am running an organization whose budget is in the tens of millions. I need to increase my financial acumen if I am going to lead well."

You don't have to have an MBA to understand the basics of accounting and finance, although it helps. This short book is a primer that will give you and those in your organization some basic tools for making smarter business decisions. Like many of my senior team colleagues at the time, many people believe that finance is the responsibility of the Chief Financial Officer (CFO) and perhaps a few staff accountants. Over the years, I have learned that we all need to understand some of the principles of accounting and finance as well as some best practices.

In our experience, most strategic leaders do not have formal training in accounting and finance. This is not their fault; it is just reality. The terminology and financial jargon tend to make it an intimidating subject to understand. Sometimes, people mistakenly believe that the accounting and finance field involves complicated math. We'll let you in on a secret: if you can add, subtract, and divide, that is all you really need — welcome to the club! Understanding financial statements is sometimes compared to learning a foreign language, but it is really not that difficult. In this book, we take the mystery out of the numbers and the accounting jargon out of the language to equip you with the financial knowledge you need to be a strategic leader.

I [David] remember a financial presentation I once made to the board of a $40 million dollar nonprofit. I had one slide with a table of numbers and one slide with a graph of those numbers. I made a comment to the group that some people prefer to see the numbers in a table, while others prefer a visualization of the data. One of the board members leaned over and whispered to me with a smile, "And some of us prefer to skip this part!" I knew that he was joking, but I also understood that there was some truth to what he was saying: people tend to avoid financial conversations if they are not equipped with the financial knowledge to participate in the discussion. I think they avoid it for two reasons, first, they know it is very important, and second, they are afraid to show their ignorance of the subject. In our experience, most of today's leaders have gaps or misunderstandings in their financial knowledge.

Our goal in developing strategic leaders is to provide some foundational financial tools. We present these tools in simple, easy-to-understand language. Whenever we use a formal financial term, we define it in plain English.

Target Audience

For different reasons, this book is designed for both financial professionals and non-finance leaders who work at both for-profit companies and nonprofit organizations and want to improve their understanding of and decision-making with financial data. Financial professionals can use this book in working with the non-finance people in your world. Some of these non-finance individuals currently manage a budget (budget owners) and they may want to learn how to manage the budget more profitably. Lastly, this book is also helpful for financial professionals who would like to elevate their organization's financial knowledge by using the tips and recommendations in each chapter.

Here are the five strategic financial tools that all strategic leaders should understand:

1. Cash Is Your Lifeblood

Cash is like the blood flow in your body. Without cash, you cannot survive. How do you generate cash, use cash, and make sure you have adequate cash reserves on hand? Cash (or the lack thereof) is the number one reason businesses run into financial trouble. As important as cash is for an organization, it is one of the most misunderstood financial areas. Our goal is to take the mystery out of cash and move this measure to the front of your organization's financial reporting and mindset.

2. The Bottom Line

For an organization to achieve financial health, it must consistently generate more revenue than expense. The "bottom line" is simply the amount of surplus or deficit generated when looking at the organization's total revenue less its total expenses. When you have a positive bottom line, it means that you have some margin to build adequate operational financial reserves that can be used on rainy days or for new projects. Inability to manage the bottom line creates a ripple effect of financial trouble for organizations.

3. Trade-Offs: Managing Costs

Sometimes, it can be difficult to predict revenue. To ensure that the bottom line is positive, you need to manage what you have much more control over: your expenses. Organizations often say they have a revenue problem, but what they lack is the courage to rebalance and realign their expenses to fit the reality of their current revenue. Keeping expenses in line and proportional to revenue is one of the most important steps to keeping your organization financially healthy. Organizations need to look at expenses as an investment made specifically to generate a positive return. This view will go a long way in helping to make trade-off decisions in strategically managing an organization's financial health.

4. Budgets and Forecasting

Budgets and forecasts are invaluable tools for helping you and those you work with manage the bottom line. That said, they are nothing more than tools. Budgets and forecasts are not revenue or expense. They are indicators or planning tools and should not be over- or under-used.

5. No Silver Bullet

No single strategy will solve all of your financial issues. Instead, you need to find the right collection of strategies to help you and your team build financial health and strength over time. Ten strategic initiatives that each deliver a 1% improvement is much better than trying to find the one home run initiative that will deliver a 10% improvement (as tempting as that may sound). The risk of one or two initiatives not working is mitigated with the first approach. Successful organizations don't swing for the fences every time they are at bat: they consistently build financial health and spread out risk in order to weather the hard times that are sure to come.

In summary, begin by understanding the **cash flows** in your organizational "world" and develop strategies that result in positive **bottom lines**. Managing your **costs** with skill and discipline is central to this journey. **Budgets and forecasting** can help you and your team to reach these goals. Lastly, **no single silver bullet**, but rather a collection of strategies, will help you to make this happen as you advance your mission, vision, and strategic priorities.

MEET OUR ONE LEADER AND TWO MANAGERS

Throughout this book, we use fictional characters — one leader and two managers — to serve as examples for how you might use the tools presented here to benefit your organization.

Alex, Our CFO

Alex, the senior leader in this book, is an experienced CFO with an accounting degree and MBA. Although she is well-versed in both accounting and finance, she is new to this role in her organization. As Alex gets up and running, she realizes that she has about 50 budget owners and other important financial stakeholders, many of whom do not have strong financial backgrounds. She will be using this material as part of a six-month lunch and learn development sequence.

Chris, Our IT Director

Chris is the IT Director at a nonprofit organization, but could just as well be at a for-profit company. She reports to the VP of Operations and oversees a team of IT staff members as well as an IT budget of several hundred thousand dollars. She has a technical background in IT but little-to-no background in business, accounting, or finance.

Chris is an example of a non-finance professional budget owner who has the potential to build her financial acumen. In each chapter, we will talk about why the tool should matter to Chris and how she could benefit from understanding it more thoroughly. We will not only explain the main concepts of the tool and how it works, but also what Chris can do next to put this tool to use in real life.

Phil, Our Sales Manager

Phil is the Sales Manager of a for-profit company. He reports to the VP of Sales and Marketing. His profit and loss (P&L) responsibilities include meeting revenue goals as well as managing the expenses of his personnel and operations. While Phil is not a financial professional, he is responsible for several million dollars of revenue and expense.

THE CENTRALITY OF CREATING VALUE FOR STAKEHOLDERS

The starting point of nearly any endeavor is creating value. You can only understand the role of financial resources if you understand that the goal of every company and organization is to create value for its stakeholders. Creating value is providing to others something they see as a benefit. Here are some examples:

- **Personal** Stakeholders: My wife, Cheri, and I are working on visiting all of the national parks in the United States. Why? Because she is my primary stakeholder and she values visiting these parks.

- **Professional** Stakeholders: I often communicate with our MBA faculty through a short video update because they value the material but don't want to sit through another meeting.

- **Organizational** Stakeholders: We moved the Trevecca MBA program to 36 hours because those in the marketplace value a shorter program more than the traditional 42-48 credit hour format. From 2013 to 2019, our MBA enrollment has grown from about 70 students to 300.

For more information on this critical topic, read Chapter 1 of *Strategic Leaders Are Made, Not Born*.

TEMP RESOURCES

In my book, *Building Strategic Organizations*, I provide an easy-to-remember acronym for resources, TEMP. TEMP stands for:

- Time
- Energy
- Money
- People

Obviously, this book focuses on money. All resources are limited and the purpose of any resource is to advance your mission, vision, and strategy. Additionally, you should be able to track how the investment of resources has led to an important return. Return on Investment (ROI) is a cornerstone for all strategic leaders.

Return on Investment (ROI)

Return on Investment is a simple but profound concept. When you invest TEMP resources in an endeavor, you expect to get something in return. Waste occurs when you invest resources into something and see little or no return on that investment. The goal is to invest as few resources as possible to get your needed or expected outcome or return.

Unfortunately, most organizations do not look carefully at TEMP resources as investments, but they should. The decision to hire an administrative assistant for a manager, for example, should not be made simply because all the other managers in the organization have administrative assistants. Rather, the decision should be evaluated based on the potential return this investment will generate. If an assistant is hired for $40,000 plus benefits, will the department's productivity and financial results increase significantly by more than this amount? When you pay for a product or service, you expect a good return on that investment. If the product or service brings you greater value at a lower cost next year, all the better.

WHY EVERYONE NEEDS FINANCIAL ACUMEN

When children are young, their parents may teach them only the most basic financial topics, like having an allowance. As these children grow from thirteen-year-olds to thirty-year-olds, it is imperative that they learn how to manage their own financial health and future as an adult. It has been our experience that many employees (some of whom are currently managing multi-million dollar budgets) are still at this very basic level of financial understanding.

Allow me to use the example of a lemonade stand to illustrate a basic level of financial understanding. When a child runs a lemonade stand, they get an old cigar box from their grandfather and a handful of coins for making change. Each morning, they take money out of the cigar box to buy more lemonade and throughout the day, as customers pay them, they put the proceeds into the box. At the end of the week, they count how much is still left in the box to see how their lemonade business venture did.

What is wrong with the lemonade stand approach to finances? Let's unpack it. How much lemonade did you sell? How much did the lemonade cost? How much profit or loss did you make? Using the basic lemonade-stand-with-cigar-box approach, you will not be able to answer all of these questions because revenue and expenses were not recorded separately. I use this example because in my work as a consultant, I have seen this very basic financial understanding (or, I should say, misunderstanding) at all levels of organizations. It is imperative that we treat our workforce like adults and not children. If they are to lead and manage effectively, employees must move beyond a very basic understanding of organizational finance.

Financial understanding and transparency in the financial dealings of an organization are more important than ever before. Transparency works best when employees understand strategic finance. That is what this book is about. If you are a senior leader, you can provide this book to all of your employees and then spend some time with them in-person or virtually relating these tools to the life of your organization. When employees move beyond the lemonade stand understanding of finance, it is easier for everyone to pull on the same rope in the same direction.

If you have ever watched a construction team roof a house, you know that it is a big job. Every roofer on the team wears a tool belt so that he or she can work at peak efficiency. Imagine how slow and ineffective they would be if only one roofer had a hammer. Unfortunately, this is how many organizations operate financially. One employee has the financial knowledge and acumen and they run from one meeting to another to add their knowledge to decisions being made. A much better approach is to provide all employees with the tools they need in order to make the best decisions for the organization.

TRANSPARENCY

In today's world, growing transparency is generally the better policy. This doesn't mean that you have to share everything with everyone. Think through your entire workforce and consider what would be best to share with whom. On transparency, Berman and Knight (2009) write:

> Everyone is proclaiming the importance of transparency. It's mentioned in the *Wall Street Journal* almost daily and we hear it promoted in the quarterly earnings calls of Fortune 500 companies. To be financially transparent a company must present financials that an outsider can easily read and understand. The numbers should give the reviewer a feel for the strengths and weaknesses of the company. Sarbanes-Oxley is all about helping companies become more transparent.

> The benefits of sharing the numbers are tremendous, as Joe has seen firsthand at Setpoint Systems, where they have an open book philosophy. Each employee is trained to understand financial statements — shared weekly. Bonuses are tied to the company's performance.

> The employees at Setpoint feel psychic ownership — they care about how the company does week-by-week and they want to see

the numbers moving in the right direction. Financial transparency has helped Setpoint create a committed workforce. (para. 1-3)

I [Rick] direct Trevecca's MBA and DBA programs. At many universities, it is common for academic directors to have little transparency regarding overall revenue and expense. If the senior finance team wants me to care about the financial performance of my programs, they have to be willing to be transparent on some of the financial information.

MATH AND EMOTIONS

You would think that smart people would do good analysis and make good decisions. You would be wrong. Every day, smart people make decisions based on emotions rather than on math.

Joe Knight (2015) writes: "I could also tell you the story of a company owner who wanted to buy an airplane. When the CFO analyzed it and said 'No way,' the owner got another CFO" (para. 13).

In my book, *Building Strategic Organizations*, I call this "the data vs. the most powerful person in the room." After some team discussion, the senior leader can say, "I understand what the data set says, but we are going to do what I want anyway." You can probably tolerate this once in a while. If it is a common occurrence, you and your organization have a bigger problem.

Another problem that leaders have is their comfort level with making small, sometimes inconsequential decisions, and how uncomfortable they are around making large multi-million dollar decisions. During the next meeting you attend, pay attention to how much time on the agenda is spent debating whether Casual Friday should include jeans vs. the time spent talking about launching the next product. You will be surprised and maybe a little disappointed that it is not always a productive use of the team's time. I'm sure it is human nature and comfort level that causes this behavior. Almost everyone will have an opinion about what Casual Friday should entail, and making a mistake on a small decision like this will not be catastrophic for the organization. Larger decisions, on the other hand, could mean larger mistakes, but it is extremely important for leaders to increase their comfort level around these big decisions. Solid financial knowledge for all key leaders will ensure both more robust dialogue and that an appropriate amount of time is spent making the big and very important decisions.

In the accounting world, there is a principle referred to as "materiality." The principle states that accountants do not have to follow a generally accepted accounting rule for an entry that is so small that it does not make a difference in the accuracy of the financial statements. A simple example would be the following. For an organization with a billion dollars in revenue, it is acceptable for the accounting team to record a $350 airline ticket as an expense when it was purchased even though the flight is going to occur in the next fiscal year. Technically, that expense should be recorded as a prepaid expense for the company's next fiscal year, but since the amount is so small, it is not considered material enough for a billion dollar company to spend the time, energy, and effort to record the expense differently. The principle of what is material needs to be considered during meetings. Spend more time working on the big topics and less time on the small ones. In doing this, the comfort level will grow around making these big important strategic decisions that are material for the organization's future.

USING THIS BOOK

Your use of this book will vary depending on whether you are a Financial Professional (FP) or a Non-Financial Professional (NFP).

Financial Professionals
Spend some time talking with your organizational and financial leaders about what you are going to share with whom. As a financial professional, you know that the organization will generally be more successful when the level of financial knowledge increases. Increased

financial knowledge means that decisions are hopefully more data-informed and less emotion-driven.

Non-Financial Professionals

Talk with your financial leaders about what financial detail is available and what is not. If not much is available, audited financials are a good place to start. Sometimes, non-financial professionals believe that their organization's financial statements are top secret. Most of the time, this is not the case, and you can learn a lot about the organization you work for when you read through the financials. In this book, we will be giving you the tools you need to understand what you are looking at and to ask the right questions. When the decisions you make are backed up by a solid understanding of the financials, your company will be more successful. Oftentimes, this translates into your personal career success.

1.

CASH FLOW IS YOUR LIFEBLOOD

"Number one, cash is king...
number two, communicate...
number three, buy or bury the competition."

–Jack Welch, Former CEO of General Electric

"Let me ask you this question," said David as we interviewed several CFO candidates for a consulting client. "If you could only look at one of the three financial statements (Balance Sheet, Income Statement, and Statement of Cash Flows), which one would it be?"

Not being a finance professional myself, I was curious to hear how they would answer this question. All three of the candidates answered the Statement of Cash Flows. Cash is one of the most important measures in most organizations – cash flow is like our blood flow. Without it, you cannot survive.

On a different occasion, David and I were working with an organization that had run significant deficits for several years. Their auditing firm was deciding whether they were going to issue an opinion that included a warning about "going concern," meaning that there were questions about the organization's survival. Their only hope was getting an infusion of cash in the form of a several million dollar line of credit from their bank.

How does an organization reach such a point of desperation? Are there ways to prevent this? Most of the time, the answer is yes, there are ways to prevent this if cash is managed carefully.

Think of cash like a savings account. When an organization generates a surplus because it has a good quarter or year, unused funds are deposited into the savings account. When an organization has a deficit or loss, a withdrawal from savings (cash) is needed to cover expenses that revenue does not cover. Cash is an important measure of health and an organization's ability to sustain itself in the future. Cash is usually measured as an amount (or balance) at a certain point in time. For example, at the end of the month, Organization XYZ has a cash balance of one million dollars. This is different than how revenue or expense is typically measured — as an amount over a period of time. For example, Organization XYZ's revenue over the last six months is $5 million.

WHY IT MATTERS

Without cash, an organization cannot function. Organizations run out of money all of the time. They find that there is not enough cash in the bank to pay employees, suppliers, or utility bills. In fact, the number one reason businesses fail is because they run out of cash. Since cash is such an important resource, organizations that want to thrive need to pay attention to it. Of the three major financial statements — income statement, balance sheet, and cash flow — the cash flow statement is unfortunately the least understood and the least used. In fact, up until the mid-1980s, the cash flow statement was not even a required statement for public corporations. Let's take a little time to see why CFOs value this statement so highly. Cash for an organization is like the blood in your body: when you run out or it stops flowing, you die. Organizations that do not pay attention to their cash in addition to their revenue, expenses, and bottom line results could find themselves in a situation where they can no longer function.

HOW IT WORKS

Does your organization often report on its cash balance? Do senior leaders know how much cash is on hand? In our experience, cash flow is a neglected reporting and awareness area in most organizations. Cash flow needs to be more than a measure left to one or two employees in the accounting department.

Where should you begin? What should organizations be looking for when they examine their cash balance? Sometimes it is helpful to look at cash amounts in terms of how many months of operation they cover. If your organization spends one million dollars a month on employee payroll and general expenses, do you have enough cash in the bank to operate for two months, three months, or six months? Cash really is the lifeblood of the organization, and you need to know how many pints are on hand for the ebb and flow of the financial year as well as for an organizational emergency.

Cash – The Basics

Organizations get cash one of three ways: 1) generating it operationally when revenue exceeds expenses, 2) through investment activity, when investments they hold earn a return, or 3) borrowing it in the form of debt (remember, borrowed cash does need to be repaid with interest). There is a fourth way for public companies to raise cash by issuing shares of stock, but we will not delve deeply into that here.

Healthy organizations generate cash from the operation of their business. Revenue comes into an organization as a product or service is sold to customers. Expenses go out of an organization as it pays employees or purchases the materials and supplies necessary to run the business. When the revenue generated by a business consistently exceeds its expenses, additional cash will be generated. If an organization's expenses consistently exceed the revenue generated, cash is consumed. Some companies call this "burning cash" or "cash burn rates." I like this terminology because it offers a good picture of what is happening organizationally.

Why would a company "burn" cash or consume more than it takes in? I believe that there are two reasons: 1) The company is rapidly expanding into a market and is choosing a deliberate strategy to invest more than they are bringing in to grow market share, or 2) they simply don't know that they are burning cash because financial literacy is low. I remember a conversation I once had with the president of a $30 million organization after reviewing its financial statements the night before. The president was shocked, and visibly upset, that his organization had unknowingly been burning as much cash as it had for over five years.

Cash Balance

Most young people today have a banking app on their phone. They periodically open the app to look at how much is in their account. This is their cash balance. It is measured at a certain point in time. For most young adults, it is usually measured just before they get their paycheck deposited, as in, how much do I have left? Or it is measured just after they get paid, as in, how much do I have to spend? Organizations have cash balances that they need to monitor for very similar reasons.

Tip for financial professionals – Does your internal reporting contain metrics on the cash balance? This does not need to be a complicated analysis showing the various account balances where the organization's cash is kept, just a simple one-number metric. The key is to consistently measure it.

Tips for non-financial professionals – Do you know who to ask about the cash balance in your organization? Are regular financial reports that contain the company's cash balance shared with employees? Since cash is an organization's lifeblood, it is good to know how much is on hand for emergencies. Remember to keep the context of the organization in mind when you look at the number. A cash balance of $3 million might seem like a lot for your personal budget, but if you are part of a billion-dollar organization, that figure may represent only one day of typical expenditures.

Cash Flow

Cash flow is a different measure than cash balance. Cash flow is simply a measure of how much the cash balance has changed over a period of time. This is helpful to look at to gauge organizational progress toward a specific goal. If the cash balance at the beginning of the month was one million and the balance at the end of the month was one-and-a-half million, then the cash flow for the month was a gain of half a million. Cash flow is such an important measure. Most analysts on Wall Street would say that cash flow is the single largest factor in determining the share price of a publicly traded company. An important note here is that Wall Street analysts use the company's anticipated future cash flow, not the company's cash flow last quarter or last year. Sorry to burst your bubble on a great idea of how to get rich in the stock market.

Also, remember that cash flow can be uneven — or, as David Tarrant likes to say, "lumpy." For example, let's say that you have $12 million in annual revenues. Maybe some months have $3 million of revenue and other months have almost none. You have to anticipate this uneven or "lumpy" pattern so that you don't get caught with insufficient cash reserves. It is important to understand how much cash is needed and how that changes on a month-to-month basis.

Sources of Cash

Where can an organization get cash? As stated earlier, organizations can generate cash through their normal operations by managing the revenue and expense in a way that results in a surplus. Organizations can also borrow cash. Of course, borrowed cash has to be paid back, so loans are not the magical solution to all your organizational problems.

Whether you work for a for-profit or a nonprofit organization, strategically managing debt is key to your financial success. Debt is a four letter word, but it is not necessarily a bad one. Debt can allow an organization to fund a new initiative sooner than relying on internal reserves would permit. Debt can also be used in the place of funds that are currently invested and earning a higher return than the cost of servicing the debt. Debt can also be misused if an organization handcuffs itself to a very large loan that is difficult to pay off. We have seen this with nonprofit organizations where the outstanding debt is sometimes greater than the nonprofit's annual revenue. After drilling down on the reasons why these nonprofits have so much debt, it is usually a "field of dreams" reason: "build it and they will come." This behavior is very risky. It is important to think of borrowing and debt as an investment that requires a return. Borrowing that results in an increase in revenue is much better than borrowing that has no impact on the organization's ability to generate more revenue.

WHAT TO DO NEXT

Look at your organization's cash balance. Do you know where the money is? Typically, it is in a bank, but it could also be invested and less liquid ("liquid" is a financial term that describes how easy or difficult it is to access to quickly pay bills). Cash in a checking account is very liquid; cash in a savings or money market account may be less liquid (it may take days, or even weeks, to withdraw and use it to pay bills). Take some time to understand where the organization's cash is and how liquid it is. Measure how many days, weeks or months it could sustain the organization if revenue were to decrease.

For Non-Finance Professionals

For NFPs, you could ask your organization for their audited financials, which will include a Statement of Cash Flows. Remember, some financial professionals may not want to share these with you. Or, you may be at a private company that doesn't share that information. Cash flow statements are available for all publicly-traded companies. For example, if we look at Home Depot's 2017 Cash Flow Statement, we see the following:

- Net Cash Flow-Operating: $9.7 billion
- Net Cash Flows-Investing: -$1.6 billion
- Net Cash Flows-Financing: -$7.8 billion
- Net Cash Flow: $.3 billion (total of all three of the above)

For Financial Professionals

As a Financial Professional, it is good to educate your leaders and managers on the important role of cash in your organization or company. An easy place to start is by going over your cash flow statement with your leaders and managers. Include simple, overall measures of cash on hand in some of the regular financial reporting. Have conversations with key leaders and managers on whether the organization is increasing or decreasing its cash balance and what the goals are for cash. Most managers want to know how they can help or what their role is in generating cash. Break it down for them with some simple measures like these:

- Collect sooner from customers
- Stretch out payments to suppliers
- Ensure that areas of the business generate more revenue than expense
- Watch the annual expense and capital budget

Alex Leads Session on Cash

In her first hour-long session with her budget owners and other finance related employees on "Building your Financial Acumen," Alex discusses the importance of cash to the operation of the organization by providing specific examples. She also covers timing related to cash as well as sources of cash.

Checking in with Chris and Phil

For IT Director Chris, cash is important. Let's say Chris wants to make IT equipment purchases, including new computers, servers, and software, totalling one million dollars. When that contract is signed, a million dollars will go out the door. As Chris interacts with the leaders of her organization, they may have questions about the timing of that purchase and also the plan for depreciation. Chris would want to think through and talk through these two issues (timing and depreciation) to better coordinate cash flows.

As Sales Manager, Phil is very excited because his team has made a million-dollar sale. Phil needs to know the difference between when the revenue is booked (recorded) and when the cash is received. Sometimes that discrepancy could be one hundred days or more. The same is true of fundraising at nonprofits. There can be a significant lag between booking the revenue and receiving the cash.

2.

THE BOTTOM LINE

*"We expect all our businesses to have a positive
impact on our top and bottom lines ...
Profitability is very important to us
or we wouldn't be in this business."*

–Jeff Bezos, CEO of Amazon

Most everyone has heard of "the bottom line." It is important! When you consistently have more expenses than revenue, the survival clock is ticking loudly for your organization. Every organization, both for-profit and nonprofit, has revenue coming in and expenses going out. This is important not only at a point in time, but also as a trend. It is one thing to have a bottom line that is occasionally negative. It is even more significant with the bottom line that is constantly negative over time.

Let's take a look at Home Depot again. If we review their income statement from 2017, we note the following:

- Total Revenue: $94 billion
- Operating Expenses (plus interest, taxes, etc.): $86 billion
- Net Income: $7.9 billion

This shows us that there is a vast difference between "top-line" revenue and "bottom-line" net income ($7.9 billion or 8.4% of revenue). There are many companies that have billions in top-line revenue while the bottom-line shows a loss of billions. Here is an example from Uber (2017):

- Total Revenue: $7.9 billion
- Operating Expenses (plus interest, taxes, etc.): $11.9 billion
- Net Income: -$4.0 billion

We need to understand top-line revenue and the bottom line and the relationship between the two. Recently, I spoke with a long-time executive of Lamar Advertising, who reported that the most important for them was revenue. His thinking was misguided, because the bottom line is more important than the top line. Even companies that generate $10 billion in top line revenue will not stay in business long if it takes $11 billion in expenses to generate that top line revenue.

WHY IT MATTERS

The bottom line is the relationship between revenue inflows and expense (costs) outflows. Financial health is developed when revenues consistently exceed expenses. This is true at the highest organizational level as well as at the departmental or program level. Everyone across an organization should understand how their work contributes to the bottom line.

Nearly every manager has heard the term "bottom line." In fact, it is often used as a way to illustrate the main point of a discussion, as in, "Let me get to the bottom line" or "The bottom line is this..." While we have all heard the term, we are not all familiar with what it means financially.

If you work at a for-profit company that is publicly traded (meaning that shares of the company's stock are available to purchase at a stock exchange), the owners (shareholders) of the company expect bottom line profits. The bottom line is the reason the owners (shareholders) of the company have invested their money in the organization. Put another way, the bottom line is the reason the company exists, making this measure a very important one.

Why do shareholders care so much about bottom line profits? It is because these profits are what is distributed to them in the form of a payment called a dividend if the company pays a dividend. If the company does not pay a dividend, profitability and the resulting increase in cash drive the increases in the share price that equate to a return on their investment.

If you work at a for-profit company that is not publicly traded, the bottom line is just as important: the only difference is that the shareholder or owners don't offer shares of the organization on public stock exchanges.

Is the bottom line important if you work at a nonprofit? Many people mistakenly presume that "nonprofit organization" means that an organization does not place an emphasis on bottom line profits. A better term for nonprofit organizations would be "not-for-tax", or "non-taxed" organizations. Nonprofit organizations are not taxed on their profits, but they do need to generate one if they want to stay in business and continue to provide the products and services that they do. When working with finance professionals who are new to the nonprofit world, I often ask them to place a sticky note on their computer monitor that says, "not for-profit, but also not for loss." This serves as a constant reminder that while the nonprofit organization they work for does not distribute profits or pay tax, keeping their organization healthy by producing positive bottom line results is just as important. The number one reason a nonprofit gets into financial trouble is because it ignores this very important principle.

HOW IT WORKS

How long will a business be able to survive when its expenses are greater than the revenue it generates? Some businesses can sustain small losses for short periods of time because they have "savings" accumulated in the bank (as we discussed in the previous chapter, we call that a "cash balance"). Do you know whether you are generating a positive bottom line for your organization? Are your revenues greater than your expenses? If not, what is the organization's plan to fund those losses (savings in the bank "cash," borrowing money, or some other way)?

I remember a conversation I once had with the CFO of a very large nonprofit organization that was struggling to make its bottom line positive. This organization was carrying a very large amount of debt and with that, a sizeable loan interest expense. I asked the CFO about his plan for the debt. Was it part of a strategy to grow the top-line revenue and be better able to service the debt costs? Was it part of a strategy with a donor who was gifting the organization a large sum to enable them to carry all of the costs of this large loan?

As it turns out, it was neither: the President really wanted to build some new facilities as soon as possible, so rather than waiting for the organization to raise the money through donors or saving the money through operational results, they borrowed the money. I think this was a rather short-sighted decision that was now drowning the organization in the costs of servicing that debt. To use an example in your personal finances, this would be like building another garage and five new rooms on your house by adding them to your credit card. Sure, the new space is nice, but you really can't afford to make the payments. Organizations are no different from individuals when it comes to managing the bottom line. There are no secret accounting tricks that allow organizations to avoid the discipline of managing their finances to achieve a positive bottom line: it boils down to the simple exercise of managing expenses in relation to the revenue. Let's dig a little deeper into how the bottom line works by looking at some of the measures of profitability at different levels of the financial statements.

Margins

Financial statements and reports often have amounts on them referred to as "margins." The margins are measures of revenue less certain amounts of expense. Sometimes it is helpful to think of this using the example of your personal finances. In your personal budget, revenue is the amount you are paid for your job. Perhaps you want to know how much money is left over every month after certain expenses are paid like mortgage, car payments, utility bills, etc. This amount is a margin that you calculate as the paycheck revenue less these expenses. Calculating this margin might be useful if you are trying to save money for a down payment on a house or a college fund for your children. Organizations need to look at different margin measures for their strategic goals, such as paying off debt, giving employees a raise, or building a reserve for purchasing new machinery or new construction. Often, these margins are measured as a dollar amount and/or a percentage of the top line revenue. The bottom line is often referred to as the **net margin** or **net income**. This is the difference between all revenues and all expenses. Successful organizations need to manage this margin to attain a positive result.

There are also different margins that measure total revenue less different types or portions of expenses. Let's walk through a few of these and discuss how they can be valuable measures.

Gross Margin

Certain types of businesses examine a measure referred to as the **gross margin**. The gross margin is total revenue less the expenses attributed to manufacturing or procuring a product for sale. If your organization is in the widget business, the gross margin would be your total revenue less the costs or expenses only attributed to procuring or manufacturing the widgets. Expenses that would not be included in this gross margin are those related to selling or marketing the widgets or the cost of the team that runs the company.

Why is it important to look at a gross margin? When you examine gross margin over time, it can tell you many things. Is the gross margin increasing or decreasing? (It is important to look at this as a percentage of sales as well as a total dollar amount). Is the gross margin per widgit increasing or decreasing over time? Is the increase or decrease attributed to selling the widget at a different price or is it because of a different cost (or both)? Gross margins measure how much money is left over after deducting the cost of manufacturing the product to pay for the company's other expenses and still deliver a profit.

Contribution Margin

The **contribution margin** is defined as the difference between revenue and variable costs. **Variable costs** are the costs in an organization that change with the amount of product being manufactured or sold. If each widget that is manufactured requires three screws, screw cost would be a variable cost. If you manufacture 1,000 widgets, you will need 3,000 screws. This margin is mostly measured in a manufacturing business, but it can also be used for some nonprofits and service organizations.

Contribution margins and gross margins are frequently confused because they are similar, but the differences are very important to understand. Let's walk through a simple example of this powerful measure and discuss how beneficial it is in making strategic decisions using the widget business example.

The widget company manufactures widgets. The company sold one million widgets at a dollar each last year. The costs of manufacturing those widgets were as follows:

1. $200,000 raw materials to manufacture widgets
2. $100,000 labor to construct the widgets
3. $50,000 cost of shipping widgets to customers
4. $225,000 management team that leads the widget company
5. $150,000 advertising expense
6. $125,000 rent and utilities expense for the widget company building

Expenses 1, 2, & 3 are considered variable costs because they vary with the number of widgets produced. Using our example of one million widgets produced, we can calculate that each widget has 20 cents of raw material, 10 cents of labor, and 5 cents of shipping cost. The total variable cost of each widget is 35 cents. The math is as follows:

1,000,000 units / $200,000 raw materials = 20 cents each
1,000,000 units / $100,000 labor = 10 cents each
1,000,000 units / $50,000 shipping = 5 cents each

The other three categories of expense (4,5, & 6) are considered fixed because they do not vary with the number of units produced. Whether the widget company manufactures one million widgets or one widget, they will still advertise, pay the management team, and the rent and utilities for the building. Of course, one could make a solid argument that if only one widget was being made and sold for a dollar, the management team would not exactly be doing the job they are being paid for. Now, let's look at the contribution margin.

Each widget is sold for one dollar and the variable costs required to produce that widget are 35 cents. That means that every widget has a contribution margin of 65 cents ($1.00 less $0.35 = $0.65). Now that we know the contribution margin, we can make some strategic decisions.

How many widgets does the organization need to produce to break even for the year? "Break even" means zero profit, or revenue equal to total expense (fixed and variable). If every unit has a contribution margin of 65 cents and the total fixed costs of the company are $500,000 ($225,000 management team + $150,000 advertising + $125,000 rent and utilities), the break even is calculated as follows:

Total fixed cost of $500,000 / contribution margin per unit of 65 cents equals 769,230 units to break even.

Knowing the break-even volume is important because the management team knows that they need to produce and sell more than 769,230 units if they want to earn a profit.

Let's say the management team has identified a customer that would like to purchase two million widgets next year, which is the maximum amount the widget company can produce in one year running around the clock. They have made an offer to purchase these widgets at 50 cents each. Is this a good deal for the widget company?

Using the contribution margin, we can answer that question. If two million widgets are sold at 50 cents each, total revenue would be $1 million (2,000,000 units * $0.50), total variable costs would be $700,000 (2,000,000 * $0.35 variable cost per unit) and there would only be $300,000 left over to pay the $500,000 in fixed costs, leaving a loss of $200,000. Obviously, this would not be good for the widget company, but knowing their contribution margin and their costs, they can construct a counteroffer.

When considering their counteroffer, the widget company would like to earn a profit on this deal that exceeds the profit earned in the prior year. Let's look at what we know:

- Desired profit is greater than last year's profit of $150,000
- The customer is interested in purchasing 2 million units
- The variable cost for 2 million units is $700,000 ($0.35 a unit * 2,000,000)
- Fixed costs are $500,000 (remember, these don't change with the number of units produced and sold)
- The customer would have to pay an amount greater than $0.68 a unit ($700,000 + $500,000 + $150,000 = $1,350,000 / 2,000,000 units = $0.68), so the widget company will do a counter offer at greater than $0.68 cents a unit.
- Contribution margins are very important in making strategic decisions because the organization is basing their decisions on a solid understanding of their costs.

The table below contains the numbers associated with this contribution margin analysis:

Widget company	Prior Year		Breakdown		2M Offer		2M Counter Offer	
Units produced / sold		1,000,000		769,231		2,000,000		2,000,000
Price per unit	$	1.00	$	1.00	$	0.50	$	0.68
Total revenue	$	1,000,000	$	769,231	$	1,000,000	$	1,350,000
Raw materials	$	200,000	$	153,846	$	400,000	$	400,000
Labor to manufacture	$	100,000	$	76,923	$	200,000	$	200,000
Shipping	$	50,000	$	38,462	$	100,000	$	100,000
Total variable costs	$	350,000	$	269,231	$	700,000	$	700,000
Manangement team	$	225,000	$	225,000	$	225,000	$	225,000
Advertising	$	150,000	$	150,000	$	150,000	$	150,000
Rent and Utilities	$	125,000	$	125,000	$	125,000	$	125,000

Organizational-Specific Margins

Organizations can create their own margin measures that are unique to them. What are the different ways your organization might benefit by looking at the revenue and categories of expense? Here are a few suggested margins to look at:

- Revenue less sales and marketing expense
- Revenue less manufacturing expense
- Revenue less compensation and benefits expense
- Revenue for product A less the support costs of product A

The key in developing organization-specific margins is to measure what matters. If the margin helps the organization better understand itself, it is also a useful measure. If the margin helps the organization make better decisions (more strategic decisions), it is a useful measure.

The Bottom Line vs. Change in Cash

The bottom line is the difference between revenue and expense. Healthy organizations work hard to make this a positive number. It is important to remember that the bottom line is not the same as the change in cash. For a simple personal budget, the change in cash (your bank balance), might be the same as your bottom line result (your paycheck less your expenses). Most organizations have complex accounting and financial systems that require us to take a few more steps to arrive at the change in the organizational cash balance. The bottom line result is one component in determining the change in cash, but we have to factor in four other components: 1) depreciation expense, 2) capital expenditures, 3) changes in debt, and 4) changes in working capital. Let's walk through a simple example.

Grace is a non-profit organization that provides counseling services for lower-income families. Their revenue comes from a private foundation grant and from donations. Their expenses are primarily payroll for the fifty employees, but they recently purchased a new computer system for $1.6 million dollars. They also borrowed $5 million several years ago to purchase their headquarters building. The President of Grace has asked the finance manager to prepare a report that shows him why the cash balance decreased by $1 million last year, even though the bottom line on their audited income statement was a positive $0.5 million. To prepare for the report, the finance manager pulled together the following financial figures from the year that just ended on June 30th:

- Revenue - $10.0 million
- Expenses - $9.5 million
- Depreciation expense of $0.3 million - included in total expense figure above ($0.2 million of this is from the IT equipment + $0.1 million from the purchase of their headquarters building)
- Capital expenditures of $1.6 million for the technology equipment
- Principal payments of $0.2 million on a loan taken out several years ago for their headquarters building.
- Since Grace is a small non-profit, they do not have significant working capital (working capital is current assets, such as cash, accounts receivable, and inventory, less current liabilities, such as accounts payable)

Change in cash calculations for Grace last year are as follows:

1. **Bottom line of $0.5 million** - calculated as revenue of $10 million less expense of $9.5 million.
2. **Plus depreciation expense of $0.3 million** - since depreciation expense is a non-cash expense included in the total expense of $9.5 million, you need to add this back in to your change in cash calculation.

3. **Less capital expenditures of $1.6 million** - Grace wrote a check for $1.6 million to purchase the technology equipment. As soon as that check was cashed, their bank balance went down by $1.6 million. Since this is a capital expenditure, their auditors and generally accepted accounting standards have required them to spread this expense over the useful life of the IT equipment, which is seven years. The total amount of $1.6 million does not show up as expense in the first year. Instead, it shows up as depreciation expense of $0.2 million per year for the next seven years ($1.6 million / 7 = $0.2 million).

4. **Less principal payments on debt of $0.2 million** - Grace took out a loan to purchase their headquarters building. Last year, they made a payment on that loan of $0.3 million ($0.2 million was principal and the remaining $0.1 million was interest expense). The interest expense portion was included in their total organizational expenses, but principal payments are not expensed on the income statement. Because the principal portion of $0.2 million was an outflow of cash, it needs to be considered in the change in cash calculation.

5. **Plus / minus changes in working capital $0 million** - Grace is a small nonprofit without inventory or accounts payable accounts. Because of this, the change in working capital (current assets less current liabilities) is zero. For manufacturing companies, you will want to factor in changes in working capital when working through a change in cash example.

Grace's finance manager presented the following report to the President to show why their cash balance decreased by $1 million dollars.

Grace - change in cash balance report (in millions)		
A) Bank balance prior year end	$	1.7
B) Current year revenue	$	10.0
C) Current year expense	$	9.5
D) Bottom line (B-C)	$	0.5
E) add back depreciation	$	0.3
F) subtract capital expenditures	$	(1.6)
G) subtract principal payments on loan	$	(0.2)
H) Total change in cash (D+E+F+G)	$	(1.0)
I) New cash balance (A+H)	$	0.7

WHAT TO DO NEXT

Take some time to list your organization's sources of revenue and sources of expense. Have any of these sources changed over time? Is the long-term (five or more years) trend upward or downward? Expenses often exert upward pressure on organizations with little control over them. Employees expect raises, supply costs sometimes go up, and employees usually have very little incentive to control costs because that often involves additional work or work behavior change. Pay careful attention to the sources and trends of revenue. Could some sources be trending downward? Are there changes occurring that will have a significant impact on future revenue?

Alex Leads Session on the Bottom Line

Alex begins by discussing how the organization views the bottom line. This focuses on what is included and what is not. Next, Alex reviews how margin is calculated for the organization overall as well as by program, product, and service line. Lastly, she focuses on the places where fixed and variable costs come into play.

Checking in with Phil and Chris

You probably remember that Chris directs IT, which is a cost center. Cost centers are primarily an expense without revenue. They affect the bottom line on the expense side but not on the revenue side. The goal for Chris and her team is to invest in those things that are most aligned with their organization's strategy and reduce the cost of those things that bring little value to operations.

Phil's sales team is a profit center that includes both revenue and expense. They need to bring in revenue and contain expenses to create an agreed-upon margin. For example, they may need to produce an 80% margin — meaning that the sales team must bring in $1 million and spend only $200,000.

3.

TRADE-OFFS: MANAGING COSTS

"We don't have a revenue problem,
we have a spending problem."
"The essence of strategy is
choosing what not to do."

–Michael Porter, Bishop William Lawrence
University Professor, Harvard Business School

"Watch the costs and the profits will
take care of themselves."

–Andrew Carnegie, Scottish-American
industrialist and philanthropist

You can't have it all. Because every endeavor has limited resources, it always comes down to which things you should do and which things you should discontinue. Making these trade-offs is at the heart of strategic leadership. Most organizations fall into the trap of thinking that every time a new idea arises, it needs to be funded with new money. Let's look at an example of this.

Katherine is the VP of Marketing for a medium-sized organization. She has been working with her team on a new idea to advertise online using social media. After pitching the idea at the latest senior team meeting, a question arose: "How are we going to find the money to try this new idea?" Katherine's idea is not in the organization's budget and would require a significant financial outlay (almost 5% of the total annual expense for the year).

Many times, organizations do not look at these opportunities as a potential trade-off. Do we have to wait until next year to add this great new idea to the budget? Should we go ahead and spend the money, even though it is not in our budget and our organization will run a deficit for the first year before the new advertising starts to generate significant new revenue? Are these our only two options? Just as you make trade-off decisions in your personal life, such as whether to spend or save your year-end bonus, organizations need to make trade-off decisions regarding where they will spend their limited resources.

WHY IT MATTERS

Organizations need to look at all of their expenses as investments that should generate revenue (or a return), either directly or indirectly. Successful organizations do this on a regular basis and tie measures and accountability to these. Many organizations make the mistake of only looking at new expenses thoroughly when they are initially undertaken and then do not look at them again. If you start to look at expenses as investments that require an organizational return, you will see them differently, making potential trade-offs easier to make. Think about this as it relates to your retirement savings choices. Do you select a stock, bond, or investment fund without looking at its historical or potential return? Once you have committed your hard-earned money into an investment, do you continue to monitor its performance or not consider it at all? Successful investors, as well as successful companies, look at performance on a regular basis. If one stock, bond, or mutual fund is not performing as well as a potential alternative, a trade-off is made. If Katherine's idea has the potential to generate more revenue than other expenses currently in place at her organization, then a potential trade-off may exist.

Even though this is a simple idea, it is rarely used. Let's discuss how you can put trade-offs in place at your organization.

HOW IT WORKS

When looking at trade-offs, it is helpful to think of the value that is created by every category of an organization's expenses. When we use the term "value," we are referring to organizational expenses (remember, you want to think of these as investments) that consistently produce greater revenue than cost. Estimating the value created for some categories is easier than others. The value of advertising expenses or a sales team can be estimated by looking at the revenue they generate. Estimating the value of the support part of an organization is not as straightforward, but they need to be performing an important value-creating function as well. When organizations downsize, they attempt to identify expenditures that can be reduced or eliminated in order to rebalance their financial picture. When identifying trade-offs, this same approach can be used to make decisions. Let's look at a few simple examples for Company X, which wants to make room in its budget for a new advertising campaign:

1. Tony is the company's top salesperson, generating $5 million in sales revenue a year.
2. The widget manufacturing machine produces up to 2 million widgets a year, which are sold for $1 each.
3. Lisa is the company's most senior administrative assistant. She oversees all of the customer appreciation events and trains new employees on key company policies.
4. The marketing team was moved to another location five years ago to make space for a bowling alley that employees can use during their lunch hour. The rent at the new marketing location is $8,000 a month.

As you consider these examples, what information is missing? Do you know enough to make trade-off decisions?

For #1, what is Tony's salary, benefits, and bonus each year, compared to his $5 million in sales? Are his sales with the same customers every year, or does Tony generate new customer sales?

For #2, what is the cost of running the widget machine each year? Are the widgets profitable?

For #3, what is the annual cost of employing Lisa? What do her performance reviews look like each year? What does her supervisor say about her performance? Is she meeting her goals and objectives?

For #4, is the bowling alley resulting in greater employee satisfaction or retention? What is the cost of running and maintaining the bowling alley each year?

When thinking through each of these potential trade-off options, try to estimate the associated revenue, expense, and some indicator of quality to make the most informed decisions.

You Want 10 Things But You Only Get 7

A powerful lesson in life and work is that you typically don't get everything that you want. This can relate to a car, a job, or even a hire. In hiring, I often say that no single candidate is Jesus or Superwoman. You usually have to make trade-offs.

Imagine that you have three finalists for an open position at your company. None are 10 for 10, but they each bring seven things. The challenge in hiring is choosing which seven are most important. When you look at ten items on your budget wish-list or even existing items, you can't have them all. We all have limited resources. The role of the strategic leader is to accept those things that bring high value and are aligned with your strategy and eliminate those things that bring less value.

NOTE: People in your organization will often bring a passionate plea for something they value. This may be something that is of value but which is not a high priority. Other times, it is just something they want that actually brings little value.

Trim the Tail

One place to start is with a list of all of the organization's expenditures — everything from A to Z (advertising expense to that zebra painting hanging in the conference room). Now comes the difficult part: can you rank these expenses from those that contribute the most value to those that contribute the least? Reflect on which items on the list drive revenue and put them at the top of the list. Reflect on the expenses which, if eliminated, would not substantially change the revenue generated by the organization — those go at the bottom of the list. If you are a manufacturing organization and you have expenses tied to the individual products you sell, try ranking this list from the expenses tied to the most profitable products to the least. If your organization is in the service business, order expenses by those your customers value the most to the least. This is an exercise that requires some judgement and estimates. Share the list with others in your organization. Would they agree with your ranking?

After you have generated your list and had it vetted by others, start to identify what can be trimmed off the tail end of the list. You will begin to see trade-off candidates appear. Sometimes this can be expenses that are easy to control, such as a ten-year supply of pens, pencils, and sticky notes. More often than not, it will involve employees that create low amounts of value or products and services that are more sacred cows than cash cows.

Creating a Culture of Cost Savings

Most organizations' budget managers have the false impression that their budgets should increase every year. I often hear budget managers say, "We need to keep up with the cost of living." My reply is usually, "I see... how much of a change is that?"

Some years, costs do increase; other years there is a decrease. The same is true with wages. If the budget managers in your organization routinely add increases into their budgets and plans for the year, this can contribute some substantial headwinds to finding trade-offs and optimizing the company's financial performance.

Often, budget managers treat the resources of their areas as if they were at war with the rest of the budget managers in the organization. Never give up a position, or an office space, or dollars in the budget — it would be like retreating from a hard-fought battle line. When budget managers behave this way, the organization is in trouble. Instead of being at "war" with the competition, they are at war with their own troops. Leaders in organizations need to identify this kind of behavior as soon as possible and work hard to change this destructive practice. By creating a culture of cost savings and continuously identifying trade-offs in expenses, you can significantly propel your organization forward. In order to foster such a culture, you must promote and reward this behavior which runs contrary to the status quo. Organizations that are on the front lines of this type of culture change require regular cost reduction targets to be hit, but they do it in a way that does not penalize other parts of the business. For example, if one part of the business has a target (and a reward for achieving) a reduction in the cost of a product, they may also be responsible for maintaining the quality at the same time.

Using Net Present Value (NPV) to Make Trade-Offs

When deciding to make trade-offs, organizations need to estimate the value that individual expenses, projects, or investments bring to their organization. Using a tool like net present value (NPV) can help you compare these options on an apples-to-apples basis. Net present value estimates bring projects and options with varying time frames into a value today so that they can be compared. Would you rather have $100 today, or $100 a year from now? Most people value $100 today more than the promise of $100 in the future. Financial professionals refer to this as the "time value of money." If someone hands you $100 right now, that is a sure thing, whereas $100 promised in the future has some risk associated with it. $100 received today can also be invested so that it can earn some return, making it more valuable in the future.

Let's use the example of two projects to see how NPV can help assess the value of each:

Project One involves the purchase of an automated mail machine to print, fold, and insert literature into envelopes. The machine costs $55,000 and the company that sells the machine estimates that it should operate effectively for five years. After putting this machine into use, it is estimated that the company will save the $35,000 a year that they currently spend hiring an outside service called Mail Plus to do this work for them.

Project Two is the hire of a salesperson who will focus on bringing a specific product from the company's portfolio to an entirely new customer base in China. The compensation and benefits costs, along with the associated travel costs, are estimated to be $150,000 a year. The company projects that it will take three years before any sales result from this project, but in years four through year seven, sales are estimated to reach $1 million per year. After year seven, the patent will expire on this product and it is anticipated that the market will be flooded with generic offerings from other competitors that will quickly bring sales to zero.

The company only has the resources to invest in one of these projects. How do they determine which project will create the most value?

Alex Leads a Discussion on Net Present Value

Roger is the CEO of the company Alex works for. He would like to see what the estimated value of these two projects are, so he calls a meeting with the VP of Sales, Charles, and the CFO, Alex.

"Roger, how long have we worked with each other?" asks Charles as he enters the conference room.

"We are coming up on eighteen years," Roger replied. "I remember that I hired you the same year my daughter Rachel was born and she will be going to college in the fall."

"We know each other well, so why are you wasting my time reviewing this decision?" remarked Charles. "Ever since you hired Alex, it seems like every decision needs to be analyzed. It's slowing us down! Going with our gut instinct and experience worked well for us before, but now, it seems that is not good enough."

Just then, Alex entered the conference room, "Sorry I'm late," she said, "I just finished another lunch and learn session with our company's budget owners. We talked about the importance of making trade-off decisions when planning for the start of a new fiscal year." She pulled a legal pad and pen out of her bag and turned to Charles and Roger. "What did I miss?"

"Charles was just remarking that this meeting might not be the best use of his time," Roger huffed.

"Let's get to the bottom line. Isn't that what you always say, Alex?" remarked Charles. "I know the revenue from my China project will not come in for three years, but it's a million a year, *and* we are more or less guaranteed that for four years after that. Why are we talking about a stupid $50,000 paper machine? China is four-million dollars of revenue, easy."

"That's nothing compared to the savings of not working with Mail Plus," Roger countered. "Look, Alex, I like you and I know you are helping our organization understand accounting and the numbers, but we don't sell numbers. We sell products, and every minute we waste talking about the accounting numbers is another minute we are not talking to customers and selling. I don't have time for another spreadsheet. I have to see an important customer later this afternoon."

"I understand," said Alex, "I only want ten minutes of your time to talk about these two projects." She walked over to the whiteboard and began to write.

"Charles and Roger, I know your time is valuable, so please allow me to quickly show you how these two projects look financially. Charles, I agree with your estimate of the $1 million in revenue that can be gained in China, but let me remind you that that particular product has a margin of 30%, so while we may sell $1 million, we only net $300,000 every year."

"Okay," said Charles, "but $300,000 for four years is still a lot more than what we pay Mail Plus."

"You are correct," replied Alex, "but let's also remember that we have the additional expense of the salesperson on the China project and the cost of his travel and supplies back and forth to China. This is what the China project looks like and here is the resulting net present value."

"Net presents, what?" Charles looked confused.

"Net present value takes the value of the project over time and converts it into a number today that we can use to compare with the net present value of the, what did you call it? Stupid paper machine?"

"OK, kids, let's take it down a notch," interjected Roger. "Remember, we are on the same team here. Go ahead, Alex, show us the net present value of both of these projects so we can make a data-driven decision."

Alex smiled when she heard "data-driven" because it reminded her of her job interview with Roger, during which she excitedly knocked over her water bottle in his office when she waved her arms talking about the need for more data-driven decisions and fewer emotion-driven ones. Alex proceeded to quickly write these sets of numbers on the whiteboard of the conference room.

NPV Analysis - Automated mail machine	Year 1	Year 2	Year 3	Year 4	Year 5
Annual savings	35,000	35,000	35,000	35,000	35,000
Cost to purchase	(55,000)				
Project cash flow	(20,000)	35,000	35,000	35,000	35,000
NPV	**99,151**				

NPV Analysis - Salesperson in China	Year 1	Year 2	Year 3	Year 4	Year 5	Year 6	Year 7
Annual revenue	-	-	-	1,000,000	1,000,000	1,000,000	1,000,000
Cost of product	-	-	-	700,000	700,000	700,000	700,000
Margin on product (30%)	-	-	-	300,000	300,000	300,000	300,000
Annual cost of salesperson	(150,000)	(150,000)	(150,000)	(150,000)	(150,000)	(150,000)	(150,000)
Project cash flow	(150,000)	(150,000)	(150,000)	150,000	150,000	150,000	150,000
NPV	**50,982**						

"What is important to remember," Alex explained, "is that while the revenue is $4 million over four years, it is the margin on the sales that is the real financial benefit for the company. We also have to remember that it is four years of good sales, but seven years of expense tied to the sales effort that goes into this. What I do," she said as she pulled the financial calculator app up on her phone, "is to bring these projections over time to a single value today, in the present."

"Got it," said Charles. "So it is present as in 'today,' not 'presents.'"He smiled because, while he gives Alex a hard time, he likes her. She reminds him of his smart, driven, and highly idealistic daughter-in-law who is a physician with County Medical.

"I am going to use a rate of 5% to value these future contributions," said Alex, "because 5% is what the company currently pays for its long-term debt. Even though the automated mail machine is a smaller project, the savings start to show up a little more than a year and a half into the project and continue for a total of five years."

"Hold up," Charles interrupted. "How do you know that the savings show up after a year and half? Is that one of those accounting tricks?"

Alex shook her head. "No. If you take the cost of the automated mail machine and divide it by the annual savings, you get a number that is called payback. That's the amount of time it takes for the company to recover (or pay back) the original cost of the machine. It looks like this: (55,000 / 35,000 = 1.57 years)."

Roger and Charles stared at the whiteboard for a few minutes as the light went on for them. "Wow, I never would have thought that an automated mail machine could benefit our organization more than a major sales initiative in China. Let's move forward with the 'stupid machine,'" Roger laughed.

For Non-Finance Professionals

For NFPs, there are many online net present value templates that do the math for you. It is beneficial to get used to how these work and how changing time frames, discount rates, and the overall numbers can give you different net present value figures for projects.

For Financial Professionals

As a financial professional, you may have noticed that we kept this example very simple. If you are a for-profit company, you will want to consider the impact of depreciation expense and taxes in these two projects, but I think you will find that this analysis is still directionally accurate. We used 5% as the discount rate, but you will want to consider using your organization's cost of capital, or a risk adjusted rate, to discount the cash flows.

WHAT TO DO NEXT

First, go back and review the "Trim the Tail" section above. Next, as it says, list out a group of expenses and assess which one brings more value than others. Think about reducing or eliminating those things that bring less value. Again, this is about trade-offs. Nearly everything has value, but some things bring more value than others. Given the reality of limited resources, sometimes low-value things have to be trimmed.

Alex Leads Session on Trade-Offs and Costs

At her lunch and learn session, Alex stresses that every organization has limited resources. She then gives some examples of why Project A might be a better choice than Project B based on strategic alignment, ROI, as well as NPV and break-even analysis. Alex discusses how managers should work up short, one-page, strategic initiatives (also called project mini-charters) which provide an overview of financial features. It is important for Alex to be patient when working with employees who have limited financial knowledge. Employees are often excited to share an idea that might save their organization $10, when in the big picture, it is faced with a $1 million shortfall. Smile, encourage them, and continue to look for other trade-off ideas. Ten dollars down, $999,990 to go.

Checking in with Chris and Phil

When it comes to IT investments, there is no end to the money you could spend. The goal for Chris and her team is to spend an amount that fits within their organization's budget while seeking the highest possible return on their investments. They must make careful decisions about the right investments and then be able to explain the returns that came with those investments.

Phil in sales has the same issues and more. Phil needs to know what investments in personnel, programming, and advertising need to be made that will result in increased sales. Again, this is about trade-offs and margins. He may want to hire a new salesperson (or, in a nonprofit, a fund-raiser) at a cost of $75,000 in salary and $25,000 in related benefits, for a total of $100,000. Phil must then decide on the return he expects on that investment. If the new salesperson brings in $100,000, they probably aren't a good investment. If they bring in $500,000+, they are a better investment. The math is different when you are talking about hiring an office manager at $50,000 plus $15,000 for related benefits. That is mostly a cost equation.

4.

BUDGETS AND FORECASTING

*"The goal of forecasting is not to predict
the future but to tell you what you need to know
to take meaningful action in the present"*

–Paul Saffo, Technology Forecaster

Every leader should be able to develop and manage budgets effectively. Budgets, forecasts, and plans need to be directionally accurate, not perfect. Many organizations treat their budget like it is the most important objective they have, devoting far too many resources and time to developing what is really just a measuring stick. Other organizations operate without a budget at all. The smartest organizations are in between these two examples. Estimate as accurately as you can, within a reasonable amount of time, with a reasonable portion of your resources. At the end of the day, it is better to have your employees serving customers and carrying out the real work of your organization than to have them developing the perfect measuring stick.

WHY IT MATTERS

Does your organization prepare a budget? Is it an annual measure, quarterly, or monthly? Within your organization, who is tasked with preparing the budget? How much time do they spend preparing the budget?

My first job out of college was in the business planning department of a large holding company with three lines of business. Each year, hundreds of employees were involved in the planning process. I quickly realized that they dreaded this activity because they did not feel it was a good use of their time. They were right. The plans were prepared, not as a guideline or measuring stick, but to make their line of business look better than the other two lines of business. Why? So they could get the attention and resources of the parent company. At the end of the year, attention had already shifted to the next year, rather than to how accurate the current year's plan was, so it wasn't even a good measuring stick. In short, it was not a good return on the investment of time and money it took.

As a young, naive college graduate, I asked my boss about this planning process, wondering whether it was the best use of the company's human resources. He encouraged me to talk to my counterpart at another large manufacturer in town so that perhaps I could get some better ideas of how to create business plans. At the time, I wondered why my boss had a strange smile on his face (I later found out that he used to work for the other company and was thus well aware of their approach to planning).

I got in touch with an analyst at the other company, who explained that they had a special name for their internal planning process: "Hell Week." During that time, the company brought all of their key managers into the corporate office for a week of fighting over the company's limited resources. They gathered in a huge boardroom, where they reviewed the plans and ideas created by each division. The loudest voices won capital and expense dollars for their divisions by promising better performance than the other divisions.

There are much better ways to plan, budget, and forecast than a survival of the fittest contest, or a process that promotes your line of business while throwing your co-workers' lines under the bus. Let's discuss a few more data-driven, rather than emotional, approaches to planning.

First, let's take a step back here and ask: What is a budget?

A budget is an organization's (usually) annual plan that maps out its estimated revenues and expenses. Budgets are typically prepared in consultation with individual managers, who are responsible for using them as their guide for spending throughout the year. Properly-prepared budgets fit into the plans for the organization as a whole to achieve its desired financial results for the year. Some organizations prepare extremely detailed budgets that dictate how many paper clips a department can purchase that year. Other organizations take last year's budget and bump it up or down a few percentage points, depending on how they feel the revenue will come in that year, to balance out the expenses. Some organizations set a budget and refuse to deviate from it throughout the year, regardless of what their top line revenue looks like.

Smart organizations know that an annual budget is part-plan, part-guideline, part-constraint-on-spending, and one big part-educated-guess. After participating in the planning process for over 30 years, my observation is that organizations tend to spend too much time obsessing over small parts of the budget and not nearly enough time on the larger parts of the budget where a little more planning energy could yield some good returns. Let's unpack this idea a bit as we explore how it works and discuss a few techniques for how to go about planning and budgeting for your organization.

AND HOW IT WORKS

Take some time to list out the people in your organization who are involved in the budgeting and planning process. Together with the senior team, answer this question: How does the budget or forecast add value or help our organization?

For some organizations, the budgeting and planning process is simply to create a spending constraint for employees and individual departments — i.e. "We can't spend more than the budget each year." Other organizations create a budget because it is an exercise that they have always done, even though it is not well understood. Challenge your organization to look at the budgeting and forecasting process differently. How can this process help us understand our organization better? How can this process help us manage our resources better and create greater value? How can we group organizational investments in people and supplies together and compare them with the revenue they generate?

Some companies call it a budget, some use the term "plan," some call it a "forecast." Some look at one year, while others use multiple years. Some organizations do an annual twelve month budget and a five year strategic plan. While working for a large consumer products company, I got a lot of insight into what I refer to as the "planning obsession." The company would develop an annual budget like a lot of firms do, but then they would update the budget with a forecast. The first forecast was called Forecast One, followed shortly by Forecast Two, then Three...you get the picture. There were some years when ten to twelve different variations of the budget were developed, tracked, and discussed within the company. With all the hours we spent comparing one one measuring stick to another, only to throw it out to create another one, who had time to manufacture and sell products?

How does your organization plan and budget? Ask yourself — do my customers care that we have a plan or budget? Do our employees value the budget and budget process? The answer to both is probably no, but before you ditch the budget process, remind yourself of the value that the budget creates. When done correctly, budgeting and planning should help your employees engage with the financial part of the business, whether they are an engineer, an accounts payable clerk, or the vice president of human resources. Budgeting and planning also helps to put a framework and measuring stick together to help navigate through the year. No organization wants to reach the last month of the year and discover that it did not set aside an adequate amount for payroll expense. For many companies, the plan is also an important part in determining bonuses and raises, so don't scrap it altogether: recreate it so that it becomes an educational measuring stick for the entire organization. Let's look at a few ways to make that happen.

Using Last Year's Results to Prepare This Year's Budget

Businesses that are in a stable market can save some time and energy preparing their budget by using the prior year as a framework for creating the new budget. The key to doing this successfully is to have robust conversations about what is changing and include that in the new budget. This is also where the trade-off exercises can be beneficial, allowing you to identify which expenses can be eliminated to make room for new initiatives. If your organization uses the prior year to develop its new budget, make sure that a culture does not develop around a "spend it or lose it" mentality as the end of the year approaches. We have seen this behavior among many budget managers, who push to spend the remainder of their budgets as the end of the year rolls around so that they aren't stuck with a smaller budget next year. This year-end spending is rarely value added for organizations.

I had the chance to observe this "spend it or lose it" behavior first hand when I worked for a large consumer products manufacturer. The company followed a process each year of developing a budget for new capital equipment at its various manufacturing facilities. The budget was an annual amount of almost $200 million dollars. A typical year saw first quarter spending of about $20 million, second quarter spending of about $30 million, and third quarter spending of about $50 million. During the last quarter, there was always a rush to push through the last of the budgeted amount of $100 million.

The CFO once asked me if I had any good cost savings ideas, to which I replied, "Sure, I think we can save almost half of our $200 million capital budget!"

"What are you thinking?" he asked.

"Change the capital budget to a quarterly budget," I explained. "Even if it is spread evenly at $50 million a quarter, we will change the behavior of the fourth quarter push to spend the remaining capital budget."

He smiled, but the change was never made. While I realize that my proposal may not have resulted in $80 or $100 million in savings, it would have at least addressed the year-end "spend it or lose it" push. Think about the rush in your organization to spend the rest of the budget at the end of the year. What easy ways can you change this behavior by spreading the budget differently?

Zero-Based Budgeting

I think many organizations have heard of the term "zero-based budgeting," but very few do it because it requires more effort than simply tweaking last year's budget. Simply put, zero-based budgeting is done by having stakeholders start with a blank piece of paper or spreadsheet and then adding what is essential, followed by what might be helpful in creating greater value for stakeholders and the organization. This technique does not rely on historical figures, but rather treats every expenditure as if it were brand new and justifies the expense (even if it has been on the budget for decades). Zero-based budgeting can take some time, but the exercise can help your organization gain more insight into its expenditures.

Rolling Budget or Forecast

In a rolling budget, a company continually adds time periods to the end of the budget in an effort to keep it more of a living document. For example, when David and I used a rolling budget at Crown College, we would present a 3-year budget to the Board every year. When the current year's budget was approved, we would add another year at the front end. If you look at the 4x12 in the Appendix, you can also roll this over each year so that your five years back and five years forward remain current.

Closest to the Pin

On the TV game show *The Price Is Right*, contestants try to guess the price of products. The contestant whose guess is closest to the actual price without going over wins a prize.

Some companies treat their budget like *The Price Is Right*. When this happens, employees catch on quickly and realize that it is OK to spend less than the budget they submit, but they can't go even a one dollar over or the buzzer will ring and they will be out of the game. Guess what kind of behavior this incentivizes? Yes, the dreaded "sandbagging." Budget owners "pad" their budgets a little here and there because they know the organization will not allow them to go over, even by a dollar. Our strong recommendation when creating and managing budgets is to encourage the budgeting behavior of "closest to the pin". If you have ever participated in a golf scramble, or a charity golf event, you may have participated in a contest where the golfer who gets the ball closest to the hole (or pin) on their first shot wins a prize. Some golfers hit the ball a little short of the pin; some are a little past the pin. Neither of these matters because the winner is the one closest to the pin. When budgeting, it is better to have your employees estimate as accurately as possible than to have them pad a budget because they are afraid of going over, even if it is by a dollar.

A Word About Depreciation

Most financial statements have an expense line item called "depreciation" that creates a lot of confusion for non-financial professionals. Truth be told, there are a lot of financial professionals out there who do not clearly understand what depreciation is and why it belongs on the financial statement, either.

When a company purchases a building or a large machine (accountants call these "assets") that will be used over many years in the business (accountants call this a "useful life"), the expense of that asset needs to be spread out or recognized over its useful life. Because the entire purchase price of the asset is most likely paid for in the year it is bought, depreciation expense is the way the organization records each year's portion of the purchase price on financial statements instead of the entire cost of the asset in the first year. Let's look at an example.

A widget company purchases a widget painting machine for one million dollars (it's a really nice one). The engineers of the widget company and the seller of the painting machine agree that the painting machine has a useful life of ten years. The widget company purchases the painting machine for $1 million and writes a check for that amount. Because the widget company will use this painting machine for the next ten years, it would not be accurate to show the $1 million expense only in the first year and then not show any expenses for the next nine years. This is where depreciation expense is used. Instead of recording an expense for the $1 million purchase price in the first year alone, this $1 million expense is spread out over ten years as $100,000 ($1 million / 10 years) a year of depreciation expense. It is important to have a basic understanding of depreciation expense because as a non-cash expense (in accountant lingo, a non-cash expense is one you don't write a check for each year), it has a different impact than a typical expense. Depreciation expenses are present in every business that purchases assets with useful lives of more than one year. The most important thing to keep in mind with a depreciation expense is that since it is a non-cash expense, it should not be included in the organization's calculations of cash or cash flow (more on this later).

Moving to a Monthly Budget Process

When David took over as the CFO for our college, the first thing that he did was to move our annual budget process to a monthly process. Prior to this switch, nearly the only time we had operational clarity on finances was when our auditors left after the year was over. David emphasized the need to have "directional clarity" each month. This meant that our numbers didn't need to be perfect, but they needed to tell us generally what was going on at the end of each month.

In our consulting work, we often see organizations that guess their way through the year. We encourage them to make some estimates on their revenue and expenses and then use a monthly process going forward.

WHAT TO DO NEXT

Learn how much your organization invests to create a budget or forecast. List out the benefits of the budget. Does it help in decision-making? Does it help in allocating resources (people, money, time) to organizational goals? Remember that your customers don't care about your organizational budget or forecast — it adds no value for them. What they care about is your product or service. Does your budget or forecast help your organization increase its value to your customers, or is it just an internal exercise to control spending?

Discuss what would happen in your organization if you did not change the budget from year to year. How about replacing the budget with a goal like "reduce spending by 3% and increase revenue by 5%?" Some organizations occasionally do a zero-based budget. While taking the time to justify each and every expense, whether marketing or office supplies, can be time-consuming, it can help your organization gain more insight into its expenditures.

Moving to a Monthly Process

If you don't have a monthly process now, you can look at your monthly revenue and expense projections over the last few years. If you get an average of 30% of your revenue in December each year, use that as an estimate for this year going forward. You can then develop a 4x12 with your annual revenue and expenses broken down for each month.

Alex Leads Session on Budgets and Forecasting

Alex begins by reviewing the organization's budgeting and forecasting processes. She highlights the benefits of using monthly forecasting over annual forecasts. Next, Alex covers several timing issues related to budgeting, including:

- Why to backload budgets.
- The difference between required and discretionary budget items.
- Why budgets are tools to help in finances and not real money.
- The need for surplus in budgets each year.

Checking in with Chris and Phil

Chris and Phil both have budgets to manage. Chris does this well by not only preparing her budget strategically, but also forecasting her costs accurately. Phil, on the other hand, has some issues. He often calculates his expenses first and then alters revenue numbers to come up with the required margins. When things unfold, Phil often doesn't meet his revenue numbers and the whole thing works out poorly.

I once had a VP ask me why the sales projections rarely worked out positively. I suggested that they discount their budget numbers to obtain a more accurate picture. Alternatively, one could also back-load some of the sales expenses and then see how the revenue numbers look.

Lastly, we want to encourage Chris and Phil to begin using a monthly 4x12 so that they are forecasting their revenue and expenses for the year ahead on a monthly rather than annual basis.

5.

NO SILVER BULLET

*"There is no silver bullet.
There are always options
and the options have consequences."*

–Ben Horowitz, American entrepreneur, blogger

Operating an efficient and effective organization is always a trade-off and balancing act of resources. There are no magic accounting tricks to turn around a business that is losing money. Your finance and accounting staff do not have the "one solution" to make all the finance problems go away. It boils down to hard work and, oftentimes, moving many small "levers" rather than one large one. Profitability and success can be as simple as trimming in a few places and investing and growing in a few others.

There is no silver bullet. In other words, there is no one strategy that will create financial health. As with physical health, several good practices are needed to build financial strength. Here are a few of the best practices:

- Transparency
- Communicating
- Monthly Strategy Review (MSR)
- Holding back on future expenditures
- Using last year's revenue for next year's forecast

WHY IT MATTERS

After working for over thirty years supporting different organizations in their financial decision-making, I [David] can say that the financial area is still a mystery to most employees. I think the terminology and the math intimidate individuals. Many people believe that by moving numbers around on a spreadsheet, their organization will magically become financially healthy.

I like to put things in simple (sometimes overly simple) terms. There are really only three ways to improve financial performance: 1) sell more, 2) at a higher price, and 3) spend less. When revenue is greater than expenses, financial health increases. Selling more for a greater price increases revenue (so does just one of the following – selling more at the same price, or selling the same amount at a greater price). Spending less reduces expenses and helps create that margin (difference between revenue and expenses).

When I worked as the finance director of a Fortune 500 consumer products company, I learned a tremendous amount about finances and human behavior. In senior team meetings, no one ever raises their hand in the middle of a financial discussion to admit that they are confused or that there is something they do not understand. Instead, they quietly nod their heads. I have had a few brave, very senior executives come back to my cubicle after a meeting to ask some of these basic questions: David, when we talked about contribution margins and operating leverage, what did that mean? Can you help me understand the difference between the variable cost of a product and the fully loaded cost? I love these conversations because I know that there is a strong correlation between financial knowledge and business success.

HOW IT WORKS

I have also observed that in many organizations, leaders tend to spend more time on the small tactical areas they have greater comfort with.

Launching a new product line is chock full of unknowns and risks. Debating whether employees should be allowed to wear jeans on Casual Fridays — well, now everyone has an opinion they would like to share in detail. The added plus is that if something goes wrong with Casual Fridays, it is easier to change than that multi-million dollar product line launch.

Transparency

How transparent are your organization's financial figures and goals? I'm not talking about those detailed accounting reports intended for the financial professionals that can only be understood by a few people — I am referring to a few simple revenue, expense, and cash figures. Some organizations don't want their financials to be transparent because they don't want to distract employees from doing their day-to-day jobs. I think this is a mistake. Ask yourself the following question: Without transparency, do employees naturally believe that their organization is doing really well or do they think that senior managers want to hide bad performance?

Organizations with greater transparency tend to do better for a few simple reasons: 1) they foster greater trust levels, 2) employees work together to achieve financial goals or targets, and 3) because human nature tends to equate a lack of transparency with bad performance, not good performance.

Communicating

The number one employee complaint in every organization tends to be linked to communication. No matter how much and how hard an organization works to communicate, employees are critical if the message is not what they wanted to hear. There are no easy answers to this problem, but organizations that are more open and transparent tend to be criticized less for their communication efforts. However, messages sent are not always messages received.

Monthly Strategy Review (MSR)

As was mentioned before, leaders tend to have more comfort with tactical decisions — those related to the here and now — than with strategic decisions — those aimed at future success. Having monthly strategy reviews can help organizations and their leadership teams focus on what is important. Think about how to structure this kind of review meeting with your teams. Set the ground rules for keeping the conversation strategic, rather than tactical. One way to stay on track is to list the tactical topics that come up on a separate agenda to be discussed in another meeting. Strategy reviews should push the boundaries. Ask the hard questions. How can we grow our revenue by 10%? What investments would we need to make in order to double our business in five years? Strategy reviews can be an exciting time for exploring the wonderful world of "what if?" For more on using a Monthly Strategy Review (MSR), you can refer to the Appendix found in our book: *Building Strategic Organizations: The First Five Tools for Strategy and Strategic Planning.*

Holding Back on Future Expenditures

It is much easier to spend money than it is to delay an expenditure. Have you ever heard an employee comment, "I have to use up my budget before the end of the year, otherwise I will lose that money"? Or, even worse, "I have to spend my entire budget or next year I will receive less"? These can't be the best financial decisions for an organization.

As I mentioned earlier, I spent over eight years of my career working for a very large consumer products manufacturer. One of my responsibilities was managing the capital budget for factory improvements. I quickly noticed that over half of the entire budget was spent in the last quarter of the year. Get those project requests in before the year ends, boys, because there is no guarantee the funds will be there next year! During a meeting, the CFO of the corporation asked all of the analysts whether we had any cost savings ideas. I raised my hand and said, "I know how we can save a hundred million dollars! Change the capital budgeting process to a monthly or quarterly amount to minimize the end-of-year rush to get projects funded." Unfortunately, my simple suggestion was not implemented. No one believed that changing a process could result in holding back on future expenditures. The moral of the story is this: don't be afraid to make those changes to control expenses — they can have a significant impact on the bottom line.

Using Last Year's Revenue for Next Year's Forecast

It's almost human nature to believe that revenue will continue to increase each year. If your organization sold 1,000 widgets for $1,000 each last year, your revenue was $1 million. What's better than selling 1,000 widgets? Selling 1,200 widgets. What's better than selling them for $1,000 each? Selling them for $1,200 each. Now your revenue is $1.44 million. Be careful with this method of setting the budget for revenue. The problem is that higher revenue can be used to justify a higher expense. There is nothing wrong with budgeting a higher revenue number if you are reasonably confident that you will achieve it — so much so that you will increase expenses in expectation that the increased revenue will cover it. Another approach is to budget (at least to start with) the same number as last year. If revenue does increase, you can always change the budget (yes, you **can** change a budget number during the year — remember, it is *your* budget). The reason we recommend taking this more conservative approach is that it is so much easier to spend more when revenue is favorable than it is to cut spending when revenue is unfavorable.

WHAT TO DO NEXT

If, as we explained in this chapter, there is no silver bullet, but rather several things that can help you develop financial health, you can begin by looking over the following to see where you might start.

- What can you do to boost your revenue?
- What can you do now to ensure that your expenses will be less than your revenue?

- How can you reduce the cost of your vendors?
- How can you reduce your debt servicing costs?
- Are you currently carrying out any activities that bring less value than most of your other activities?
- What could you start doing to add greater value to your endeavor?

Not all of these will apply to your situation.

Alex Leads Session on Silver Bullets

"No one thing will lead our organization to financial health and strength," explains Alex. She lays out the 3-5 most appropriate strategies for the organization.

Checking in with Phil and Chris

Chris is regularly active in putting together a number of IT strategies to deliver value to her organization while managing her expenses well. We all wish we had more people like Chris who:

- View their work strategically.
- Bring vision as to what could be possible.
- Know how to make strategic trade-offs that maximize value for internal and external customers.
- Are focused and disciplined in the execution of their finance and operations.

Phil, on the other hand, brings more challenges because:

- He thinks his budget is real money.
- He pays vendors more than he should for the value that they bring.
- He is not clear on what activities bring more value.

CONCLUSION

As you work through these five tools, we hope that you are building your own financial acumen as well as that of your team. To continue the process, feel free to work through the Appendices that follow. The 4x5 and the Glossary can provide you with some additional tools and vocabulary that you can use in your everyday work.

Building financial literacy across an organization takes time and effort. Begin with yourself and the team that you lead before branching out to other departments. You can also partner with your CFO on a plan forward. In supporting these goals, you might want to do a 5-6 session lunch and learn sequence, providing a copy of this book to attendees. In the first session, start by providing an overview of the journey and introduce the quiz as a "before" exercise. Over each of the next five sessions (plan for one per month), discuss one of the tools, using examples from your organization. If you are a CFO, consider doing a similar series with your budget owners. Perhaps you could end the sequence by having your team take the quiz again in order to show them how much they have learned.

Lastly, if there is anything we at ClarionStrategy can do to help, please let us know. For some, a half-day in-service with your team might be beneficial. For those seeking a more extensive engagement, David Tarrant can work up a 4x12 for your organization and then continue building the financial capacity of your team going forward. Our hope is that you and your team can thrive in the days ahead!

APPENDIX A:

ACCOUNTING AND FINANCE QUIZ

1. What is the relationship between cash and profits?
  A. Bottom-line profits are one component in determining cash.
  B. A profitable year will always have a positive impact on cash.
  C. An unprofitable year will always have a negative impact on cash.
  D. All of the above

2. How does depreciation expense affect cash?
  A. Depreciation expense reduces cash.
  B. Depreciation expense is a non-cash expense so it has no impact on cash.
  C. Depreciation expense increases cash.
  D. None of the above

3. Which financial statement contains revenue, expense, and the difference between the two?
  A. Income statement
  B. Profit and loss statement (P&L)
  C. Statement of operations
  D. Statement of activities
  E. All of the above

4. Which of these changes increases an organization's cash balance?

    A.   Increase in accounts receivable

    B.   Increase in inventory

    C.   Increase in accounts payable

    D.   All of the above

5. The balance sheet contains which of the following?

    A.   Assets

    B.   Liabilities

    C.   Equity or Net Assets

    D.   All of the above

6. Which of the following is true about an organization?

    A.   Assets are what you own

    B.   Liabilities are what you owe

    C.   Neither of these are true

    D.   Both of these are true

7. Organizations that value financial health should avoid debt.

True - After all, "debt" is a four letter word.

False - If it is used carefully, debt can be a strategic tool for enhancing the financial health of an organization.

8. Cash flow statements are not as important as income statements and balance sheets.

True - The income statement shows important bottom line profits.

False - Cash is your lifeblood.

9. An organization's budget process should:
  A. Take a significant amount of organizational time and resources.
  B. Be completed as soon as possible by the accounting department.
  C. Be treated as an important step in developing a measuring stick that will help the organization achieve its objectives for the year.
  D. None of the above.

10. Understanding strategic financial principles is best left to the accounting and finance department.
  True
  False

11. Can a profitable company run out of money?
  Yes
  No

12. Which of the following is not found on the balance sheet?
  A. Revenue
  B. Inventory
  C. Property Plant & Equipment
  D. Equity

13. Which of the following is not found on the income statement?
  A. Accounts Payable
  B. Accounts Receivable
  C. Debt
  D. None of the above

14. Net Present Value brings future cash flows into a single value in today's dollars.
   True
   False

15. Contribution margin is the difference between revenue and fixed costs.
   True
   False

16. Gross margin and net margin are the same for organizations that do not pay taxes.
   True
   False

17. Nonprofit organizations differ from for-profit organizations in the following ways:
   A.   Nonprofits cannot legally earn a profit.
   B.   Nonprofits pay larger dividends to their owners.
   C.   Nonprofits are not taxed on earnings.
   D.   All of the above.

18. Large capital purchases should be expensed in full the year they are purchased.
   True
   False

19. Since depreciation expense is a non-cash expense, organizations can decide whether or not they want to include it in the financial statements.
   True
   False

20. When employees have a good understanding of finance, which of the following is true?

    A.   They can make better data-driven decisions.

    B.   They can spend money without supervision.

    C.   They can add greater value to the budgeting process.

    D.   They can make their own accounting entries.

    E.   A and C are true.

Quiz Answers

1. Answer A - Bottom line profits are a component in determining cash flow and changes in the cash balance. Financial results for the year can be profitable or unprofitable, but other components that determine cash flow are capital spending, changes in debt, and changes in working capital.

2. Answer B - Depreciation expense is a non-cash expense, so it does not have an impact (positive or negative) on cash. If the bottom line result includes depreciation expense (and it should), organizations need to adjust for this when determining the cash flow or change in cash balance.

3. Answer E - All of these statements are different names for the financial statement, which details revenue, expense and bottom line (the difference between the two).

4. Answer C - An increase in accounts payable increases cash because the organization has a larger outstanding amount owed to suppliers. Increases in accounts receivable and inventory consume cash and therefore decrease the balance.

5. Answer D - All of the above. Balance sheets contain all of these components. Equity is an ownership measure in a for-profit company and net assets are the ownership measure in a nonprofit organization.

6. Answer D - Assets list what an organization owns: cash, inventory, raw materials, buildings, and equipment. Liabilities are a list of what the organization owes to others, accounts payable, and short- and long-term debts.

7. False - Debt is a financial tool. When used strategically, it can enable an organization to invest and grow in ways that may not be possible if it relied only on its own operational cash.

8. False - Cash really is an organization's lifeblood.

9. Answer C - Budgeting is important. Organizations should dedicate the appropriate amount of resources to developing a budget that will measure their progress in achieving their goals.

10. False - Organizations that want to succeed train their key managers in strategic finance so that they are equipped to make the best decisions.

11. True - Profitable companies can run out of money (cash). This can happen if sales made on credit are not collected promptly and/or if they make large capital purchases that they cannot afford

12. Answer A - Revenue is not found on the balance sheet, it is found on the income statement.

13. Answer D - None of these are found on the income statement.

14. True - Net Present Value does value future cash flows in today's dollars using a discount (or interest) rate. Remember, those future dollars are not worth as much as today's dollars, therefore, they must be discounted.

15. False - Contribution margin is the difference between revenue and variable costs. The "contribution" in contribution margin is how much that margin contributes to covering fixed costs.

16. False - Gross margin is revenue less cost of goods sold, while net margin is revenue less all expenses.

17. Answer C - Nonprofits are not taxed on earnings. Nonprofits may not pay dividends, but if they do not earn some "profit," they will not exist for long.

18. False - Large capital purchases are depreciated and the expense is spread out over their useful lives, not expensed in full the first year.

19. False - Depreciation expense must be included in financial statements. It also needs to be included in the budget for future years.

20. Answer E - While a good understanding of finance is necessary to compete in today's business world, it is best to have accountability and internal controls on spending and leave the accounting entries to the accountants.

APPENDIX B:

FINANCIAL ACUMEN AND FISCAL DISCIPLINE

With skill and insight, you can develop a great plan for personal health and fitness, but without discipline in execution, your plan will not be realized. In the same way, you can have a growing financial acumen that helps you understand the best principles and practices, but you have to have the discipline to put them into action.

"John, you have been working with this senior team on developing their financial acumen and fiscal discipline. How are they doing?" I [Rick] asked.

John replied, "Their financial acumen is low but getting better. Their fiscal discipline is mixed. Some of the VPs are disciplined in what they do, while others just want to overspend every day."

You can go to the gym and work up a plan with a personal trainer. That plan only works if you demonstrate some discipline in consistent execution. Financial acumen and fiscal discipline work the same way.

Nonprofit organizations sometimes think that financial discipline is not really necessary or important. Nothing could be further from the truth.

I remember meeting with one of the senior leaders of a $30 million nonprofit organization to review his department's budget. It was clear that this vice president was not comfortable with the financial half of the organization. At one point in the conversation, he blurted out, "I'm not good at this budget stuff; I'm good at what's important!"

It was clear from his comment that he, like a lot of leaders and managers, saw the financial half of the organization as a necessary evil. The reason we refer to this as the financial "half" is because we believe that both the service side and the financial side of a nonprofit are equally important.

When she worked for the Daughters of Charity, an agency dedicated to helping the sick, aged, infirm, and poor, Sister Irene Kraus once quipped, "No margin, no mission." Sister Irene believed that strong fiscal management, not just charity, was what modern healthcare organizations needed to fulfill their missions. Charity was not enough to sustain a mission in the twentieth century. "In the United States in this day and age," she would say, "the way to do it is to run institutions that are financially solid." Sister Irene did that well enough to be inducted into the Health Care Hall of Fame.

APPENDIX C:

THE POWER OF THE 4X5/12

I have learned a lot of useful things from David over the years, but one of the most powerful has been the 4x5/12, which covers four key areas over 5-10 fiscal years. This simple 4x5 can be used to calculate new product or service lines as well as new departments or programs. This methodology can be taught to team leaders and employees, ultimately helping everyone as proposals are developed.

SIMPLE 4X5 FOR A NEW PROJECT

Assumptions
In building out a 4x5 for a new project, begin with volume, rate, and price assumptions. This gives you a feel as to the scope and size of your endeavor. For example, let's say you have a tutoring service. You estimate that you will have 40 students per week on average at one hour per week for 50 weeks at a rate of $35 per hour. Let's assume that your cost will be $20 per hour for your tutors.

Revenue
Once you have your assumptions, you can draft your revenue projections. If you have 40 students at one hour per week at $35 each, your revenue projection would be $70K.

Expense
Your assumptions can also help you calculate some of your expenses. You will also have additional expenses. In this example, expenses total $58K.

Net Income

Once you have your assumptions, revenue, and expenses in place, you can calculate your bottom line. Below is a simple example:

New Project (4x5)		FY1	FY2	FY3	FY4	FY5
Volume/Rates						
	Students per week	28.00				
	Student Rate per hour	$ 35.00				
	Tutor pay per hour	$ 17.50				
	Hours per week	2.00				
	Weeks per year	50.00				
Revenue						
	Tutoring Fees	$ 98,000.00				
	Revenue Total	$ 98,000.00				
Expense						
	Tutor pay	$ 49,000.00				
	Rent	$ 12,000.00				
	Depreciation	$ 5,000.00				
	Total Expense	$ 66,000.00				
Income from Operations						
	Earnings before Interest/Taxes (EBIT)	$ 32,000.00				
Other Expenses						
	Interest	$ 5,000.00				
Income before Taxes		$ 27,000.00				
	Income Taxes (30%)	$ 8,100.00				
Net Income						
	Net Income from Operations	$ 18,900.00				
Changes in Cash Flows						
	Income from Operations	$ 18,900.00				
	+ Depreciation	$ 5,000.00				
	- Capital Expenditures	$ (25,000.00)				
	- Principal Paid	$ (5,000.00)				

4X12 FOR EXISTING ORGANIZATIONS

This same framework can be used in larger organizations. The 4x12 represents the same four areas on the left:

- Assumptions (volume, rates, and pricing)
- Revenue
- Expenses
- Net Income

Instead of using five fiscal years, as with the 4x5, we use 12 years, including:
- Five years of back history
- Five years forward of forecast
- Two columns for this year (budget and actual)

I still remember when David became our CFO. At the time, our board was used to looking at budgets that were 20-30 pages in length. When he came in with a one-page budget and a few pages of supporting detail, the board was thrilled. In a consulting engagement we had, David put together a 4x12 for the CEO. He said in response, "This is the most financial clarity I have had in seven years." The organization's board was equally impressed.

David used to say to me, "Rick, it doesn't matter if it is a $200K organization or a $2B corporation, it always goes on one piece of paper."

There are two simple ways to get started on this. For the 4x5, just take any project you are thinking of doing and lay out your 4x5 on a legal pad or simple spreadsheet. I have hundreds of new MBA students do this in their first course each year.

For the 4x12, take the last five years from your organization's history, two columns for this year, and then five years forward of forecast. If that is a little too overwhelming at first, just go three years back and forward.

Percent Change

An additional feature you can add to your 4x5 or your 4x12 is a "percent change" column out to the right. You can do a simple spreadsheet calculation where you increase each fiscal year going forward by the percentage you put in.

Existing Dept/Org (4x12)	FY-5	FY-4	FY-3	FY-2	FY-1	Budget	Actual	FY1	FY2	FY3	FY4	FY5	%Chg
Volume/Rates													
Students per week	$ 40	$ 40	$ 40	$ 40	$ 40	$ 40		$ 42	$ 44	$ 46	$ 49	$ 51	5%
Student Rate per hour	$ 35	$ 35	$ 35	$ 35	$ 35	$ 35		$ 36	$ 38	$ 39	$ 41	$ 43	4%
Tutor pay per hour	$ 20	$ 20	$ 20	$ 20	$ 20	$ 20		$ 21	$ 22	$ 22	$ 23	$ 24	4%
Hours per week	$ 1	$ 1	$ 1	$ 1	$ 1	$ 1		$ 1	$ 1	$ 1	$ 1	$ 1	
Weeks per year	$ 50	$ 50	$ 50	$ 50	$ 50	$ 50		$ 50	$ 50	$ 50	$ 50	$ 50	
Revenue													
Tutoring Fees	$ 70,000	$ 70,000	$ 70,000	$ 70,000	$ 70,000	$ 70,000		$ 76,440	$ 83,472	$ 91,152	$ 99,538	$ 108,695	
Revenue Total	$ 70,000	$ 70,000	$ 70,000	$ 70,000	$ 70,000	$ 70,000		$ 76,440	$ 83,472	$ 91,152	$ 99,538	$ 108,695	
Expense													
Tutor pay	$ 40,000	$ 40,000	$ 40,000	$ 40,000	$ 40,000	$ 40,000		$ 43,680	$ 47,699	$ 52,087	$ 56,879	$ 62,112	
Rent	$ 18,000	$ 18,000	$ 18,000	$ 18,000	$ 18,000	$ 18,000		$ 18,000	$ 18,000	$ 18,000	$ 18,000	$ 18,000	
Total Expense	$ 58,000	$ 58,000	$ 58,000	$ 58,000	$ 58,000	$ 58,000		$ 61,680	$ 65,699	$ 70,087	$ 74,879	$ 80,112	
Net Income													
Operating Income	$ 12,000	$ 12,000	$ 12,000	$ 12,000	$ 12,000	$ 12,000		$ 14,760	$ 17,774	$ 21,065	$ 24,659	$ 28,584	

BUDGETING WITH THE 4X12

When David and I worked together, we updated our 4x12 twice a year for our board meetings. As every six months goes by, you will often have better clarity on your forecasting for the next 3-5 years. Your board will then always have directional clarity on where you are headed.

APPENDIX D:

ACCOUNTING AND FINANCE: THE DIFFERENCES

For many of us, it is unclear how accounting and finance are the same and different. In this section, we will lay out some of these differences.

Bookkeeping and Bookkeepers

Bookkeepers are responsible for keeping records of an organization's financial affairs. Bookkeepers may have an accounting degree or simply some training in how to record a business's revenues and expenses.

Accounting and Accountants

Accountants differ from bookkeepers because they are responsible for more than just making entries in a financial ledger. Accountants interpret, classify, analyze, report, and summarize financial data. Accountants prepare the financial statements for an organization and work with external auditors to certify the accuracy of these statements.

Finance and Financial Analysts

People commonly confuse finance with accounting because both areas work with financial data. Accounting encompasses more of the day-to-day tasks of ensuring the integrity of the financial statements, while finance is concerned with the organization's longer-term planning, budgeting, and financial strategy. The finance function takes the accounting data and analyzes it to develop plans and strategies for the organization's future growth and health, as well as to support decisions about how, when, where, and how much to invest in the business.

Managerial Accounting and Financial Accounting

If you have been following us thus far, please be patient with this next part, where we will use accounting and finance interchangeably. Thus far, we have explained that the accounting function is at the ground level of the forest, keeping track of individual trees, how many there are, how tall they are, and what kind of trees there are. Finance, meanwhile, is flying over the forest and looking just over the tops of the trees. Finance looks ahead at the weather, the mountains, and the forests owned by other companies. Finance makes recommendations on how to manage the company's forest, how to help the trees grow faster or stronger, and when to harvest some of them.

The accounting department plays a very important role in preparing financial statements and in providing data for analysis and managerial decision-making. When accounting is working on the financial statements, it is called financial accounting. When accounting is providing data to support managerial decision-making, it is called managerial accounting. In large companies, there are teams of accountants that support the financial statement side of the business and teams that support the managerial decision-making side of the business. In small- to medium-sized companies, there may only be a few accountants that do both. It is important that these smaller teams understand the strategic financial side of the organization so they can be better prepared to support decisions.

Tax Accounting

In large-to-medium sized for-profit businesses, there may also be individuals or teams dedicated to understanding the complexities of taxes. If a large for-profit company is also a multinational one (a company that does business in multiple countries), understanding the taxes is critical. Good tax accountants are skilled in complying with all tax regulations that the company faces. Really good tax accountants will help an organization minimize its tax liability by making strategic decisions on where to manufacture its products.

Role of the Controller and the Chief Financial Officer (CFO)

An organization's Controller is its chief accountant. This individual is responsible for all of the accounting systems and processes as well as the construction of accurate financial statements. The CFO provides oversight to the Controller and is responsible for all of the assets of the organization, helping to provide guidance on strategy and decision-making. In larger organizations, the CFO will also be responsible for other key business functions, such as human resources, risk management, insurance, accounts receivable, accounts payable, purchasing, banking, and investment.

APPENDIX E:
FINANCIAL REPORTS

Income Statement

An income statement is one of the three important financial statements used for reporting a company's financial performance over a specific accounting period, with the other two key statements being the balance sheet and the statement of cash flows. The income statement, also known as the profit and loss statement, statement of activities, statement of operations, or the statement of revenue and expense, primarily focuses on the company's revenues and expenses during a particular period.

Balance Sheet

A balance sheet is a financial statement that reports a company's assets, liabilities, and shareholders' equity at a specific point in time. It provides a basis for a company to compute rates of return and evaluate its capital structure. It is a financial statement that provides a snapshot of what a company owns and owes, as well as the amount invested by shareholders (for public companies). It is used alongside other important financial statements, such as the income statement and statement of cash flows, to conduct fundamental analysis or calculate financial ratios. The balance sheet is also referred to as the statement of financial position, or the statement of financial condition. It is important to note that the balance sheet reflects key financial account balances at a specific point in time (the end of the month, quarter, or year).

Statement of Cash Flows

This is sometimes the most difficult statement to understand and read, yet it is critical to an organization's financial health. The statement of cash flows, or the cash flow statement, is a financial statement that summarizes the amount of cash and cash equivalents entering and leaving a company. The cash flow statement measures how well a company manages its cash position, meaning how well the company generates cash to pay its debt obligations and fund its operating expenses. The cash flow statement complements the balance sheet and income statement and is a mandatory component of a company's financial reports.

APPENDIX F:

GLOSSARY

The following section defines some terms that will be helpful in building your financial literacy. If you have a few minutes, glance down through the list and pick out a word or two that you don't know. We have used plain English and a little bit of humor to define these terms. For all of you hardcore accountants out there, please forgive our irreverence.

Accounts Payable - A liability on the balance sheet, it lists and sets a dollar value for what is owed to others. Examples include what is owed for last week's delivery of raw materials as well as the electric bill that is due tomorrow (you'd better pay it if you want to keep the lights on).

Accounts Receivable - An asset on the balance sheet that lists and sets a dollar value for what others owe to the company (typically, this would be what your customers owe for the goods and services they have purchased from you).

Accrual Accounting - Most organizations use accrual accounting. This method matches revenue and expenses together to get an accurate picture of financial performance during a period of time. Large expenses are "accrued," or spread out over their useful lives, and revenues are recognized in an appropriate fashion so that the reader of the financial statement gets an accurate picture of the organization's financial health. Because Enron played fast and loose with this, it got them into trouble. Smaller organizations may not use accrual accounting because they do not make large purchases of capital equipment or because it is not important for them to "accrue" expenses. These smaller organizations use the cash method and record revenue when it is received and expenses when they are paid.

Assets - Assets are listed on the balance sheet and represent what a company owns. Typical assets are inventory, buildings, and equipment, while non-typical assets are things like "goodwill" (a made-up word describing that a company paid more than it should have when it acquired another company and that it did not know where to list the overpayment).

Balance Sheet - One of the three most common financial reports, it states the assets, liabilities, and equity at a certain point in time (often at a year-end). Nonprofits call this the "statement of financial position."

Bottom Line - Difference between revenue and expenses, also known as net income, profit (or loss, if it is negative). Healthy companies have healthy bottom lines that allow them to accomplish their goals and weather difficulties.

Break-Even Analysis - Analysis that is done to determine how much time it takes for an investment to recover its own cost. If an organization invests $1M (that would be the cost) and earns $0.5M a year from that investment (that would be the return), the break even is 2 years.

Budget - Typically, a one-year plan for an organization that estimates what its revenue and expenses (in a fair amount of detail) are expected to be. Other terms are "forecast" or "plan." Well-constructed budgets engage the organization in a road map for success by communicating priorities and allocating resources. If done correctly, the budget process educates the organization on how the finances work and which activities are profitable and which are not.

Capital Budget - Organizations often break their budgets into two parts: 1) operating budget with revenue and expenses and 2) capital budget, with large equipment and facilities purchases. A capital budget details planned purchases of equipment and facilities that will have a useful life of two or more years and typically greater than a certain dollar amount (e.g. $5,000 or more). The reason a capital budget is separate from an operating budget is because these purchases will be spread out or accrued and shown as depreciation expense on the income statement.

Cash Flow Statement: One of the three most common financial reports, it tracks cash increases and decreases that happen through operations, financing, and investing activities over a time period (often one year).

Cash from Financing Activity - This section of the cash flow statement lists changes in debt. If an organization takes on more debt, cash from that additional debt is listed here. If debt is paid off, it is listed here. One key in looking at this section is to remember that additional debt increases cash, while paying off debt reduces cash — which runs somewhat counter to the way people usually think about debt.

Cash from Investing Activity - Organizations that hold investments such as stocks and bonds show such activity in this section of the cash flow statement.

Cash from Operating Activity - This is the most important part of the cash flow statement. This section shows whether an organization is generating or burning cash through its normal operations.

Cash, Cash Flow, Cash Balance - It's like your lifeblood. Organizations need cash to pay their bills, pay employees, and buy equipment and supplies. Organizations that have a good handle on their cash are much less likely to run into financial trouble. The cash balance is the amount of cash an organization has at a specific point in time (typically at the end of a month, quarter, or year). Cash flow is how that balance changes over time. If the cash balance has increased $10,000 from January to February, cash flow is +$10,000 for the month. Both cash balance and cash flow are important measures. Get to know how your organizational blood is flowing and how many pints you have on hand when going to war with your competitors.

Common Stock - Shares of a public company that are sold to commoners like you and me. Owners of common stock have voting rights and can vote for members of the board of directors. Most common stock owners simply hold the shares of common stock as an investment and ignore the proxy (voting) paperwork that is sent to them.

Contribution Margin - This is the margin left over to cover fixed costs. Contribution margin is the difference between revenue and variable costs (costs that vary with the amount of product being produced). Contribution margins are useful in making strategic decisions around how much product to produce and sell as well as what price to sell it at.

Cost/Benefit Analysis - This is a generic term for analysis that is done to support a decision. In such an analysis, the benefits (typically revenue) are compared with the costs (typically general or capital expenses). See Net Present Value for another type of cost/benefit analysis.

Cost Center - This term is used to describe a department or grouping of expenses within an organization that provide support but do not generate revenue. The Information Technology department is typically considered a cost center because it contains technology expenses, like computer equipment, salary for IT nerds, and miles of cable, but does not typically generate revenue.

Cost of Goods Sold - This is a term that describes the direct costs that go into manufacturing a product. Typically, this would be raw materials and manufacturing labor. Costs of goods sold would not include over-head or the costs incurred in advertising and selling the products.

Controller/Comptroller - Both of these positions describe the chief accountant in an organization. "Controller" is what the cool kids call it these days. "Comptroller" is an older term that is only used by government agencies that still send each other messages using the tube system they used to have at bank drive-through windows. The next time you visit the Department of Motor Vehicles, look for the tubes right behind the Comptroller's office.

Current Assets - Current assets are assets that are currently cash, or which are expected to be converted to cash within one year. These would include cash balances, certain accounts receivable balances, inventories, and marketable securities. Contrary to popular belief, assets that are not expected to be converted into cash within one year are not called stale assets — they are referred to simply as "assets."

Current Liabilities - Liabilities that are expected to be paid to creditors within one year. This would include portions of debt that are due within the year, lease, and other payments due within one year. This could include a lease on a car or mortgage payments.

Current Ratio - This is a ratio that compares the current asset balance to the current liability balance. If the ratio of current assets to current liabilities is greater than one, it is inferred that the company has the ability to pay its short-term debts with the short-term assets on hand. Current ratios are best used when looking at the trend over time rather than just one year.

Debt Ratio - This is the amount of total debt compared to the total assets of the company. There are no hard-and-fast rules on how much is too much or too little debt — it varies from industry to industry. Obviously, if an organization's debt ratio was 1.0, that would mean debt is equal to that amount of total assets and, if you owned shares of that company, you might want to be looking for the exit door. Companies that are still starting up might have high debt-to-asset ratios, which may be acceptable if their plan is not to remain in this perilous position.

Depreciation - One of the most misunderstood financial terms. Depreciation is the portion of an expense that was spread out (or accrued) in the financial statements because of the purchase of a capital piece of equipment or a building in a previous period of time. For example, let's say you bought a truck last year for $50,000 with a plan to depreciate the amount across five years. The simple depreciation would be $10,000 per year. Depreciation is a non-cash expense (which sounds so much better than saying that it is not a real expense!). Without the use of depreciation expense to spread out a large capital purchase, the financials would be distorted. The year in which the purchase was made would contain too much expense, while the years following it would have too little expense. Take some time to wrap your head around depreciation expense — not only will it make you look smarter, it will also help you make better decisions.

Dividend - a sum of money paid regularly (typically quarterly) by a company to its shareholders out of its profits (or cash reserves). Not every public company pays dividends — typically, dividend payers are more mature companies that do not need to reinvest those funds for growth purposes.

Direct Cost - Direct costs are costs directly tied to a particular product being manufactured. Raw materials and labor used in the manufacturing process are considered direct costs. The opposite of direct costs are indirect costs, also known as overhead: shared costs not directly tied to the manufacture of the product, but in support of the organization. The human resource department would be an indirect cost for an organization because it supports all employees, not just those who are manufacturing a particular product.

Directional Accuracy - This is a term we use in planning to describe the degree of accuracy we hope to achieve with a certain process. Sometimes, managers get caught up in using an Excel spreadsheet to forecast future sales down to the penny. Even though a spreadsheet will give you as many decimal places as you ask it to, we do not recommend this approach. Our recommendation is to consider what you are estimating and make sure that you are spending the appropriate amount of time being accurate. Remember, projections, budgets, and plans are just more technical words to use in business than "guess," but at the end of the day, they are still guesses. If the projections you make are down to the penny, you may inadvertently give an illusion of accuracy in your plans that simply does not exist. It is far better to use ranges of estimates with round numbers than to use what your first pass on the Excel sheet tells you. Directional accuracy is also helpful when deciding how to spend your time developing a plan. Can you research how many pencils were used in your department, by person, by month, to put together the most accurate pencil budget ever? Yes, you can. But should you do that? Absolutely not! Rather than skipping lunch again, you workaholic, just provide a directionally accurate office supply budget.

Earnings Before Interest and Taxes (EBIT) - For-profit companies use a standard profit measure of earnings (or profits) before deducting interest expense and taxes because these amounts differ widely from organization to organization. EBIT is often measured as a percent of overall sales or as a per-share figure.

Equity - A dollar value representing ownership in a company, also referred to as "shareholders' equity." This is the amount of money that would be left over if all of the company's assets were liquidated (sold) and used to pay off all of its liabilities. Equity is used in various financial ratios like return on equity or equity per share. In a nonprofit organization, net assets are essentially the equity figure.

Expense - Expenses, expenditures, costs, and charges all mean the same thing: a company's financial outflows. Typical expenses include payroll and benefits expenses for your employees and utilities such as electricity and water. If the firm you work for outsources a lot of work to other companies, then the outsourcing cost is an expense. Expenses are typically easier to control than revenues, but can involve a far more emotional decisionmaking process when reducing expenses means that layoffs need to occur.

Fiscal Year: A calendar year runs from January to December. A fiscal year can run for any twelve-month period an organization decides. For example, many companies have a fiscal year that starts on July 1 and ends on June 30.

For-Profit Companies: This includes small, single-owner companies (sole proprietor), privately-held companies (no stock), and publicly-traded companies (with stock). For-profit companies have a goal of producing profits for their owners, who have invested their personal funds into them.

Future Value - This is a financial term that estimates the value in the future for a dollar amount today that grows at a certain growth rate or interest rate. At a 10% rate of growth, the future value of $1.00 a year from now is $1.10.

GAAP - This is the abbreviation for "Generally Accepted Accounting Practices." Instead of saying, "This the way all the other accountants record this kind of a transaction," accountants use the term GAAP to confuse people.

Gross Profit Margin - Gross profit margin is revenue less the cost of goods sold. This is the amount of money left over to cover the company's other expenses, such as advertising, sales, and overhead costs.

Income Statement - One of the three most common financial reports that tracks income, expenses, and net income over a period of time (usually one year). Nonprofits call this a Statement of Activities.

Liabilities - In the simplest sense, liabilities are what a company owes. Examples would include debt payments, utility bills, or other obligations, like lease costs. These liabilities are listed on the balance sheet to show what the organization "owes" at a certain point in time.

Indirect Costs/Allocated Costs - Costs or expenses can be categorized as direct costs (directly applied to the product or service) or indirect costs (shared costs across many products, services, or the entire organization). Indirect costs should be allocated (or spread) across the products or services being analyzed. You can use many methods to allocate indirect costs, including percentage of revenue or number of employees, but the goal is to spread them in a way that best represents the time, energy, and effort these indirect costs require to support the product or service.

Internal Controls - Internal controls are processes and procedures that organizations have to ensure the integrity of their financial and accounting information. Internal controls are in place to prevent the misappropriation of company assets, fraud, or embezzlement.

Inventory - Inventory is the term for the goods available for sale and raw materials used to produce goods available for sale. For the widget company, inventory consists of the completed widgets being held waiting to sell and the raw materials required to manufacture the widgets.

Materiality - The materiality principle states that an accounting standard can be ignored if the net impact of doing so has such a small impact on the financial statements that a user of the statements would not be misled. This principle can be applied to how material a decision is, or how much time should be spent on issues that are not material to the organization.

Net Income - Net income is revenue less all expenses. This is also referred to as the bottom line or profit (or loss, if it is negative).

Net Present Value - Net present value (NPV) is the difference between the present value of cash inflows and the present value of cash outflows over a period of time. NPV is used in capital budgeting and investment planning to analyze the profitability of a projected investment or project. See the chapter on using net present value to value trade-offs for more information.

Nonprofit Organizations - A nonprofit organization is a business that has been granted tax-exempt status by the Internal Revenue Service (IRS) because it furthers a social cause and provides a public benefit. These organizations are allowed for the public good and are not taxed. Nonprofits are run by boards and they do not have owners or shareholders like for-profit organizations.

Operating Budget - Organizations may break their budgeting into two parts. One part is referred to as the operating budget, which contains details on the expected revenues and expenses. The second budget is the capital budget, which contains the large planned capital purchases. Examples of capital purchases include equipment and facilities that have a useful life spanning two or more years (see capital budget for more detail)

Owner's Equity - This is a term that describes the funds that an owner puts into a business.

Present Value - This is a financial time value of money term that describes the value of a future sum of money in today's dollars. An interest rate (also called a discount rate) is used to convert a future value into a present value. The value of $107 a year from now has a present value of $100 at a 7% discount rate. Time value of money terms are a very important part of business strategy and project analysis, and there is value in taking the time to learn these important concepts (do you see what I did there?). Excel spreadsheet formulas on time value of money are very easy to use, but keep in mind that Excel treats cash outflows as a negative value and inflows as a positive value. See also "net present value."

Profit-and-Loss Statement (P&L) - See income statement, also known as the statement of activities for a nonprofit.

Profit Center - Large organizations create smaller units to better manage the individual pieces and parts of the company. These departments or pieces are either made up of just expenses or revenue and expenses. Profit centers have revenue and expenses, while cost centers only have expenses. Examples of profit centers include the sales department or an individual product line, such as the widget department.

Profit Margin - This is the amount by which revenues exceed expenses for a business. If revenue is 100 and expenses are 95, then the profit margin is 5. If expenses are greater than revenues, then the organization is experiencing a loss, not a profit. Organizations that are profitable can put together strategies to achieve their goals of expansion, improvement, and healthy growth. Organizations that are experiencing a loss must focus on survival, which is stressful for employees and not nearly as fun as growth.

Return on Investment (ROI) - This is a metric or ratio that compares the expected or achieved gain to the amount invested or spent to get that gain. A simple example is when a company buys or invests in a machine that produces Product X. The return on the investment is calculated as follows:

Let's say the cost of the machine is $1 million and the gain is a profit of $1.2 million on Product X. The return on investment would be $1.2M - $1.0M or $0.2M. Often, the return on investment is shown as a percentage of the original investment, which would be 20% or ($0.2M / $1.0M). Another way to think about this is by using the example of purchasing shares of stock. If you buy one share of Tesla (TSLA) and invest $400 of your hard earned money, if it goes to $500 a share, your return on that investment is $100, or $100 / $400 or 25%. If the price of TSLA dips to $300, your return on investment is -$100 / $400 or (-25%). It might be better to stick to manufacturing Product X.

Return on Assets (ROA) - This is very similar to return on investment above except it looks at a total company return on all assets, not just one asset. Return on assets is a measure of profitability and it is calculated as return / assets. Typically, a company uses net income as the numerator (the number on top) and total assets as the denominator (the number on the bottom). Net income / total assets.

Rolling Budget - With a rolling budget, an organization adds a month or quarter to the end of their budget after a month or quarter is completed on the front end. Rolling budgets are continually updated and can thus be difficult to maintain. For companies with consistent revenue and expense from month to month, rolling budgets can be a good budgeting technique to use. For organizations with lumpy results from one month to the next, they can be a headache. Rolling budgets are more common in college textbooks than in the business world.

Shareholders' Equity - This is similar to owners' equity, but the owners are a collection of individual shareholders in the company. The current value of the funds that they have invested in the company are reflected in this figure, which can be found on the balance sheet. Shareholders' equity can be calculated by taking total assets less total liabilities. If a company is doing well, this dollar amount grows because the company is earning a return on its operations.

Revenue - These are the financial inflows of a company. Revenue is also referred to as sales.

Silver Bullet - if you have a problem with werewolves, silver bullets are very helpful. If you have a business problem, it is better to spend your time looking for the right combination of strategies than to waste it looking for a grand-slam-home-run-silver-bullet solution that will take care of all of your problems. Remember: silver bullets are for werewolves, wooden stakes are for vampires, and the right combination of strategies are for your business challenges.

Statement of Financial Position (Balance Sheet for Nonprofits) - See definition of balance sheet. There is no difference between a nonprofit organization's statement of financial position and a for-profit organization's balance sheet.

Transparency - How open and transparent is an organization in sharing their financial information? Are employees given financial statements? Do cost center budget owners see how their cost center fits into the whole picture? Can profit center owners clearly see how what they do matters? Transparent organizations recognize that their trade secrets are what they do to get the financial results, not the results themselves. Employees that see the entire picture are more engaged and have a better handle on what matters and what is material. When facing a $1 million shortfall, do you want employees working on using less paper clips to do their "part", or would you rather have them pulling the levers of sales, expense, inventory, accounts payable, and accounts receivable to make a million-dollar difference?

Working Capital/Net Working Capital - Working capital is the difference between current assets and current liabilities. This net result is the amount of funds (or capital) that the organization has to invest and grow. The best way to think about this is to use the example of your own personal finances. At the beginning of the month, if you have $5,000 in your checking account because you just got paid, that is your current asset. Current liabilities are all of the bills you need to pay this month (mortgage, utilities, groceries, dog groomer, etc.). If all of your liabilities (what you owe) are less than $5,000, you have some working capital to go out to eat or go to the movies. If your current liabilities are greater than $5,000, you may want to re-think that great idea you had about getting another dog.

Zero-Based Budgeting - If you take out a clean sheet of paper every year when constructing your annual budget, you are doing zero-based budgeting. Zero-based budgeting forces the organization to look at revenue and expense (although mainly this is aimed at expense) as if it were brand new every year. Budget owners have to justify every subscription, purchase, employee, and outsourced process when constructing a zero-based budget. Because this represents such a large amount of effort, organizations rarely do a zero-based budget. It sounds good in a financial textbook, but you do not see it used much in reality. A better process is to engage your employees in a budget process that continually looks for trade-off opportunities and rewards performance improvement. Budget owners who are always looking for opportunities to improve perform much better than those who are simply defending the status quo.

APPENDIX G:

FOR-PROFIT AND NONPROFIT ACCOUNTING

I [David] have spent about two-thirds of my career in the for-profit world and the last third in the nonprofit world. There are only a few key differences between the two in how accounting is done. Generally accepted accounting principles (GAAP) are the same in for-profit and nonprofit organizations. Below are some of the key differences.

For-Profit Organizations

The name is a good descriptor of why these entities exist: to make a profit. The focus of these organizations is on the bottom line, but not exclusively the bottom line: successful for-profit organizations look at cash flow measures as well. For-profit organizations that are public have to consider that they are "owned" by their shareholders, who have purchased shares in the company to see dividends and stock price appreciation. For-profit organizations are also taxed on their profits, so managing their tax liability is also a component of good financial discipline.

Nonprofit Organizations

We prefer the term **non-taxed organizations** over nonprofit organizations because it better describes how these organizations differ from a for-profit. Nonprofit organizations typically have a mission that is designed to meet a societal need. Most hospitals, colleges, and universities are nonprofit organizations. Charities and churches are nonprofit as well.

Nonprofit organizations can solicit donations from the public and issue a receipt for those gifts that individuals (as well as corporations) can use to get a deduction from their taxes. Because of this gift component, there is a slight difference in the accounting. If a gift is received by a nonprofit for a specific use (or a specific time), it has to be kept in a separate account or fund. The accounting term for this is "fund accounting." When that specific use is met or time has elapsed, those funds are released from the separate account or fund and spent. The technical accounting terminology for that type of gift is a "restricted gift," and the accounting terminology for when it is spent is a "release of restrictions." Not too difficult so far. There is another type of restriction, and that is a permanent one. If a donor gives a permanently restricted gift, what they are in essence doing is giving a gift for which the original amount cannot be spent, but the earnings on that original amount **can** be spent. Many nonprofits have a fund called an **endowment fund** where those permanently restricted gifts are kept. The original gift amount is called a "corpus." The accounting for gifts is the main difference between a nonprofit and a for-profit.

I have frequently been asked why a nonprofit has to be run like a for-profit and achieve a positive bottom line. The answer is quite simple and it boils down to one of survival and planning. If a non-profit could perfectly plan its revenue and perfectly control its costs, then every year it could spend 100% of the money that came its way. It would not have to worry about a "rainy day," fluctuations in the marketplace, or unforeseen costs. This perfect planning organization would not have to worry about survival or creating cash reserves because it doesn't need them. Since the perfect plan is not a reality, smart organizations plan for and achieve a positive bottom line that builds cash reserves. Those reserves perform two very important functions. First, they provide a buffer for the imperfect years when revenue falls short of plan or expenses overshoot (or both). Secondly, they provide capital for opportunities that come along to make a strategic acquisition of an asset, an additional employee, or a competitor.

RECOMMENDED READING

Foundational Articles

Berman, K. and Knight, J. (2009). "Are your people financially literate?"

Berman, K. and Knight, J. (2015). "When it pays to think like a finance manager."

Knight, R. (2017). "How to improve your finance skills (even if you hate numbers)."

Foundational Books

Berman, K. and Knight, J. (2013). *Financial intelligence: A manager's guide to knowing what the numbers really mean.* Boston, MA: Harvard Business Review Press.

Harvard Business Review. (2012). *HBR guide to finance basics for managers.* Boston, MA: Harvard Business School Publishing.

Mann, Rick. (2019). *Strategic leaders are made, not born: The first five tools for escaping the tactical tsunami.*

Mann, Rick. (2019). *Building strategic organizations: The first five tools for strategy and strategic planning.*

ABOUT THE AUTHORS

RICK MANN, PHD

Rick has held a number of leadership roles across a wide variety of industries. He currently serves as Professor of Leadership and Strategy as well as Program Director for the MBA and DBA programs at Trevecca Nazarene University. In the past, he has served as the President and Provost of Crown College (MN), Director in China, executive coach, and trainer. His areas of interest and expertise begin with a passion for helping leaders and organizations access and leverage the best thinking in strategy-making and leadership development today. This extends to his research and writing in the areas of strategy, strategic planning, balance scorecards, talent management, and leadership development.

Rick has done extensive coaching and consulting with leaders, senior teams, and organizations whose budgets have ranged from $100K to $500M. Rick has an MDiv from Ambrose University (Canada), an MBA from the University of Minnesota, and a MA and PhD from Ohio State University. He is also an Associate Certified Coach through the International Coaching Federation.

DAVID TARRANT, MBA

David has worked for over 30 years in a variety of financial roles in the industrial equipment, consumer products, and higher education industries. This has given him broad experience both domestically and internationally in the for-profit and nonprofit financial fields. David loves to explain how the numbers side of a business can support strategic data-driven decision-making. He has a passion for results and finding innovative solutions to business challenges using the experience he has gained in the areas of financial analysis, strategic planning, operational excellence, and information systems.

David is currently serving as the CFO of Belhaven University in Jackson, Mississippi. In the past, he has worked as the North American Director of Finance, Pricing and Analysis for Whirlpool Corporation, the Controller of Whirlpool Canada, and various financial and analytical roles for Vickers Incorporated and Trinova Corporation. David earned his MBA from Crown College but considers himself a lifelong learner. His current interests are data analytics and repairing classic diesel automobiles.

REFERENCES

Berman, K., & Knight, J. (2009). Are your people financially literate? *Harvard Business Review, 87*(10), 28–28.

Berman, K. and Knight, J. (2009, September 8). Transparency: The buzz word in finance [Blog post]. *Harvard Business Review.* https://hbr.org/2009/09/transparency-the-buzz-word-in

Berman, K., & Knight, J. (2013). *Financial intelligence: A manager's guide to knowing what the numbers really mean* (Revised ed.). Boston, MA: Harvard Business Review Press.

Chabotar, K. J. (2006). *Strategic finance: Planning and budgeting for boards, chief executives, and finance officers.* Washington, D.C.: Association of Governing Boards of Universities and Colleges.

Christensen, C. (1997). *The innovator's dilemma: When new technologies cause great firms to fail* (Reprint ed.). Boston, MA: Harvard Business Review Press.

Christensen, C., Allworth, J., & Dillon, K. (2012). *How will you measure your life?* New York, NY: Harper Business.

Christensen, Clay. (2010). How will you measure your life? *Harvard Business Review, 88*(7/8), 46–51.

Knight, J. (2015). When it pays to think like a finance manager. *Harvard Business Review.* https://hbr.org/2015/03/when-it-pays-to-think-like-a-finance-manager

Knight, J. (2009, September 8). *Finance: What managers need to know* [Video file]. Retrieved from https://hbr.org/video/2226587631001/finance-what-managers-need-to-know

Knight, R. (2017, March 31). How to improve your finance skills (even if you hate numbers). *Harvard Business Review*. https://hbr.org/2017/03/how-to-improve-your-finance-skills-even-if-you-hate-numbers

Mann, R. (2019a). *Building strategic organizations: The first five tools for strategy and strategic planning*. Nashville, TN: ClarionStrategy.

Mann, R. (2019b). *Strategic leaders are made, not born: The first five tools for escaping the tactical tsunami*. Nashville, TN: ClarionStrategy.

Porter, M. E. (2011). What is strategy? In HBR's *10 must reads on strategy* (pp. 1-38). Boston, MA: Harvard Business Review Press.

Sinek, S. (2009). *Start with why: How great leaders inspire everyone to take action*. New York, NY: Portfolio/Penguin.